NO PARADOX

Living Both In and Outside of the Matrix

Through Consciously Evolving Our Consciousness

[Theory, Exploration, Tools]

By
Julia Woodman

previously known as the poet, artist, and magazine editor
Jay Woodman

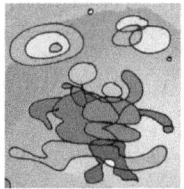 

First edition 2015
© **Julia Woodman (both text & art)**
All rights reserved.

ISBN: 1-897920-82-2
Woodman's Press
46a Marlborough Hill, Dorking, Surrey, RH4 2DD

With special thanks to my husband Chris Larn for help with editing.

INDEX

3	A Useful **Framework**
8	The **Journey**
18	**A View from Outside the Matrix**
21	A look at some **Supposed Paradoxes**
44	**Experiencing** – Transience, Witnessing, Being
65	**Exploring Altered States** of Consciousness (inc Meditation, Subtle Activism, Channelling, Shamanism, Divination, etc.)
126	The Possibility of **Consciously Evolving Consciousness**
131	The **Beautiful Simplicity** (inc Identity, Essence, Joy, Vision)
141	So **Why Are You Still Here?** (including Dropping Fear)
148	**Enhancing Our Lives** (Affirmations, Visualisations, Stories)
159	A brief look at **Handling Change**

CONSCIOUS EVOLUTION

163	**One** – Where we need to Start (Self in the World) [Loving One's Self & the World, Meditation, Higher Communication, Reminders that bring us back (Movement & Breath, Energy Management, Rituals, Guides, Nature), Gateways, Positive & Purposeful Living]
184	**Trying to be Two** (In Relationships) [Balance, Tenderness, Laughing Buddha, Self Care, Acting as if]
191	**Many, but still One** (A Place in Local & Global Communities)
197	End Notes - **Escaping the Matrix**

A Useful Framework -
to help us Consciously Evolve our Consciousness beyond present limits.

I would like to show that we can become so much more through awareness. That is why I speak of conscious evolution. If we understand ourselves, how we think and react, why we do things…. Then we can work out how to think more constructively, act more usefully, do things more easily, become more of the person we really want to be deep down inside.

The way we perceive the world around us has a great deal to do with how we react too. We all have our own views on how things look, what makes sense, what we like and dislike, what is right or wrong, etc. People don't even see colours the same as each other, so how are we to fully see how things look through others' eyes? Our world is coloured by our upbringing, by our friends, and our teachers, as well as by our own direct experience.

Some things seem to be viewed in similar ways by many people, and I think we should take another look at these and truly question them. In our search for our own truth we need to ensure we are not acting like sheep, merely following the herd behaviour.

One of these areas is that things are often regarded as opposites, things like black and white, day and night, light and dark, are obvious examples. A more open view might say they are opposite sides of one coin. I would go a little further and suggest to you that they are actually part of the same thing. Just as the coin cannot exist without its two sides, I would suggest that our world cannot exist without these so called opposites because they give us a spectrum to exist in, a matrix, or framework, that stretches between the two extremes (or polarities) to include every variation of light and shade that we sense or experience in-between.

Just as we see the spectrum of light in rainbows, or tune our radios in to some place in the spectrum of radio frequencies, we are enabled to experience life on earth because of the range of possibilities between these supposed opposites. Your experience of life differs from mine largely because of your understanding of where you are in this spectrum. If you don't think about such things at all, then you probably have views that are very black and white and your experience of life is led by those beliefs. If on the other hand you are the sort of person who understands that everyone has a right to their own views and they are bound to differ from yours yet are still equally valid, then you can see that we all have a different part to play in one huge picture. You might go so far as to say that life is good because of the huge variety of experience available to us, and that we can learn a lot from each other.

Of course our universe is not just a spectrum, it contains a hell of a lot more than x and y and positive and negative, it is multi-dimensional. So the words holograph, web or net, or matrix, are more useful.

I suggest that all conscious life may stem from a universal source of consciousness and then be separated out to experience physical life within this matrix. There are also a lot of other things in the universe that have been dreamed up either from the original source, or via conscious representations of it. We are able to add to the experience of the original consciousness that which it cannot experience directly itself (as it is too pure a form of consciousness to experience such things directly), yet it can send out its scouts as it were to check out the lay of the land and report back to it. Another analogy could be the source of a stream, where the original pool stays pure but parts of it run downstream and further and further out until droplets experience being drunk by cows, poured on plants, or passing through sewerage systems, but in the end all is recycled into rain and falls again on the hills. The journey of each part can be very different, and some journeys will be very prolonged, going round and round in mini-cycles, until eventually they are returned to the start or origin of the main cycle.

We tend to personify everything around us, including 'Gods', but I just can't believe that a 'God' could be like a person. However, I can imagine a 'God' to be a source of pure consciousness. And we would all be little parts of that consciousness. No matter how far we got separated from the original source (or stream) we would never be completely separate, there would always be some link back, no matter how tenuous it may seem at times. And I think that is all that matters….. that we go out, that we experience life, that we continue our journeys (no matter how many times we go round and round in sub-sections of that journey). I can't say for sure if we return in any form with all our amalgamated experiences, to that source, or if we feed back the experiences continually as we go, although my own experience leads me to believe that we do both. This makes me think that consciousness itself must be expanding, and that everything is interlinked, so that we can pick up on each other's ideas, knowledge, and feelings, through the ether. This makes me feel that we are all part of a team….. and capable of so much more than we generally tend to perceive. In any case, it seems to me that everything, in this world and beyond, goes in cycles, infinitely, and time and place matter not at all.

Whether we come to this view or not does not matter either. What matters I think, is that we do learn to be aware - so that we can at least consciously consider what we individually choose to think, and thereby live in whatever ways we choose to live.

What I am sure about is that the choices we make do make a difference to our lives, and those choices depend very much on our ability to be aware of everything around us and of our selves, and the possibilities we have of choice. Even those who live in very difficult circumstances have the ability to make choices that improve their lives, I have seen this many times. Even if it is impossible to change external circumstances, it is possible to change one's attitude, one's means of coping, one's quality of existence, simply through conscious attention.

If we accept that opposites (or gradations of circumstances, or differences in ways of being) are all part of the same hologram of life (just as we need different shades and colours to make up a picture), then we can see that we need all those aspects to make up our world.

The way people behave is usually just a reflection of where they are in their journey of consciousness, what their own experiences thus far have been. We do not have to react to them, we can simply move to our own level of understanding. By observing others, we can also reflect upon our selves, and our own ways of being.

If we can master our thoughts then we can choose who we show ourselves to be every moment of every day. What takes priority is not what other people think of us but what we think of ourselves. I do not mean in an egotistical way, with pride or judgement. I mean in a humble way, where we are at peace with ourselves and all around us because we know we are being who we want to be, and also because we are totally free to allow others to be whomever they wish to be. We do not need to control anything, as we do not need to depend on anything outside ourselves, therefore we cause no hurt. We are complete - with our inner link to the source of all consciousness. We can rejoice in being in the world, experiencing and witnessing in whatever way we please.

So for me the essence of life is very simple. It is just this, awareness that allows us to trust in our own truths (without feeling any need to convince others), living gracefully amidst the chaos, maintaining a sense of balance (not being pulled around by the supposed opposites or false paradoxes), and being able to choose how to direct our lives.

In this book I attempt to show ways of achieving this. I am not claiming that I am perfect, far from it, but just that I like to go on trying to be who I want to be. I attempt to show that paradoxes simply form a matrix or framework to enable us to live and experience life on this physical planet. Our minds are wonderful things, but they can very easily be tricked by such illusions, so we tend to start off living in a rather chaotic way until we gradually learn that we can step outside of this illusion enough to see it in a totally different light. Through that understanding we then become able to live in more deeply satisfying ways.

There will be detailed discussions, plus sections of tools for your further use should you wish to try them, and there will be more of these in other books, and via my website, as I continue to learn, and write.

I think that we always go on learning, and I am sure I can learn from my readers and people who attend my workshops or request support and advice. There are always new ideas, new ways of looking at things, new perspectives. I am just suggesting one way that has worked for me.

That way does stem from a belief. Not a religious belief, but a belief that, **through awareness, consciousness can and does evolve,** a belief that creation and evolution are all part of the same cycle – **as we evolve so we intentionally create better lives for ourselves, and as we create, and develop ideas, so we learn and evolve more.**

The more conscious we can be the more aware we are of what we are doing, who we are being, of whether we need to be that way or whether we might learn to change. The more aware we are, the more we can stop being buffeted about by the world out there, and through deliberate intention, create a way of BEING that works for ourselves.

By the end of the book you will be able to make up your own minds. All I hope is that you get from it the best that you wish for. Ideally, you should have some idea of the bigger picture, and thus have gained the ability to live outside (as well as inside) this 'matrix'. You should thus feel free instead of trapped, and even just that in itself should make a huge difference. It's a bit like living in a house with doors and windows instead of one with none – so you can look out from within at different views, but you can also go out and look back to check if your roof is about to start leaking or not, and explore what else is around you.

While understanding that we need this matrix to experience life on earth, we should also be able to enjoy a certain sense of detachment from it, and thus feel more empowered to make our own choices. We should thus come out feeling much more in control of our own personal journeys.

The Journey

When I was a child I always felt at one with the environment and at peace alone out in wide open spaces. I was lucky that my parents' adventurous lives enabled me indulge this in places like Ireland and Africa, and that we also talked a lot about what might be going on out in space. I guess this is about the closest we ever got to religion as kids, so it was not surprising perhaps that out of the four of us, two of us particularly developed an extremely intimate relationship with our environment, and skills that are often referred to as extra-sensory, but which we regard as quite natural. We also tend to see a bigger picture. If we aren't caught up in detail, the bigger picture can be very clear. And so we have always looked out at the universe, and beyond that, and back to the tiny space where we stand, and desired to make sense of it, not necessarily by mathematical calculation or detailed plotting, but largely by gaining an overall sense or concept of it. If you look at life from the point of view of a specialised science or a religion only, for example, then you are bound to miss parts of the equation.

I long ago reached the conclusion that everything was interlinked, out there, in here, all of us everywhere. Consciousness is the one and only answer I can come up with that explains the stream of life within us all, the creative impulse beamed out in all directions near and far. This would be the source of everything spreading outwards, evolving. So immediately we see that creating and evolving are part of the same thing. Why should the two be mutually exclusive, as the Creationists and Evolutionists tend to argue?

This is the starting point perhaps of my book. If two such things are really part of the same cycle of events…. or continuation of life, then surely other things that may appear to be opposites might also be part of one process, so I set out to examine other paradoxes.

This is the point at which I knew it was time to write this book. I actually knew when I was aged only 3, standing by the vast sea on the west coast of Ireland, that I would one day write something like this. A few years later in Africa I also remember thinking about scientific 'laws' being due to change as we discovered more. It seemed to me that I knew about science from some other place/time/experience). My journey took me round many fantastic deviations but I was always drawn back to this project. I was always finding one more bit to fit.

In more recent years I discovered Spiritual Healing, Dowsing, and a whole host of wondrous things besides, which certainly distracted me for a while, but this has been a big part of the journey too. I gradually learnt through personal experience, and through reading and research, and think that I have twigged now how the final bit of my theory works – and can see a whole big round lovely-jubbly picture. However, if we are curious, then we always go on learning more, so the adventure of life continues!

One of the earliest things I learnt was about love, that there is ultimately only love, that it completely dissolves fear or hate or any of those baser things that get in the way of loving. Oh yeah, the feelings may still come up, but we can stand back from them and catch ourselves. If we can truly just open our hearts in any situation instead of reacting in any of the other common ways, then bingo, magic happens. If you are learning this lesson, you will be tested on this over and over again and at deeper and deeper levels. When you say you can do something the universe seems to want you to show it, perhaps because it wants to learn back from you, or to witness this as a reality. Perhaps it is just to establish that you know that you know. **Once you fully get that you are part of a living natural cycle of an endless stream of life, then you know that all knowledge and experience is accessible, and for sharing.** You even stop fearing death because you know there is more than that somehow. It's not a surface knowledge like what you might have learnt to pass a test, it's a deep instinctive sense of knowing.

The other major thing is regarding the ego. The human being is a wonderful thing and it has many parts to it. We have to remember that an ego is just one of those parts that we need for basic survival type things, and not for much else. If we witness ourselves strutting our egos about then we also witness how other people cringe from it. Each person on this earth has an equal right to be loved and cherished and have sustenance, it does not matter what they do. Just cleaning work for example is as important as the next job, if not more! What ego often does is try to persuade itself that it is more important (when it clearly isn't). We should just laugh and tell it to leave it off. Great performers who work with humility are much more touching to listen to. The fact that they simply love what they do shines through. People who do fantastic work but who know it comes from the universe for everyone to share in, do far more magical things than people who try to take ownership and make demands. Humanity works as a team far better than as a group of individuals, and we are a team, we are part of the huge universal team called life. It is a shame that in our human world, the corporate, financial, and political parts of the team so often gain a position of (false) power, such that they make the mainstream or 'establishment' unpalatable to many intelligent people who end up opting out and trying to go it alone.

What life does though, this stream of consciousness dividing out and dividing out into millions of life forms, is to create ways for us to be able to experience different things. It doesn't want us to just be little ripples of consciousness coming from the big Mama and Papa waves, it wants us to sense things in different ways, so that it can begin to feel through us what life can actually be like. The big major stream of consciousness can't feel what it's like to jump and sing and dance and taste ice cream unless we do it for it. So the stream has to evolve, or change, as it divides out further and further into little strands. The main strand that gives us the Life Force, is deep within each and every one of us, and that is what gives us the link to each other and to the knowing of things about the universe that we just somehow know. Then there are these other layers which we ourselves affect….. the reality that each of us chooses to live with.

This is a pretty major thing you know. You start off as a child with a mummy and daddy if you're lucky, and they teach you things from their realities, and you maybe take those on board as part of your reality too, maybe not. At some point though you begin to notice that mum's reality is not quite the same as dad's…. dad thinks it's okay to go out every night to the pub and mum doesn't. Mum thinks kids should learn about life from having pets but dad is cross about that idea. If they'd each had one kid then maybe their realities could've stayed intact (until other influences came along), but now they have to compromise. Compromise works fine, marriages work fine, but other times they don't. Communication is the absolute key for people to work out compromises. We see what happens when people stop communicating and chuck things instead, including bombs.

So good communication is key to living in an evolved world, and here again, my model will hopefully help, as once you grasp an idea of the system, it just makes such obvious sense. Stopping to think before you start blurting out idiotic, loud, untake-backable, hurtful things, or before trying to force or manipulate people into going along with what you want, becomes so much easier when you see the bigger picture. **You automatically become more objective.** Rather than feeling as if you are being subjected to events and to other people's actions, you are able to step back before you react and thus respond more rationally. This in turn actually makes you feel more powerfully in control of your life.

So going back to the ego, this is not a good part of you to let rule your life, but it is a useful part of you sometimes, you just have to strike the right balance between these different strands of yourself. The main strand that we create is our own version of reality (built up from an amalgamation of things we learn via our upbringing and from our own experience of the world around us, but we never let go of the strand within us that links us to nature and god or love, or whatever you want to call this life giving consciousness. This is the strand you connect to in meditation, or sitting on a mountain top watching the sunset, or doing a mantra, or just humming. It is the zone you get into when practising tai chi or producing a work of art. Some people call it linking with your higher-self. It is a light and easy link or focus, not a heavy concentration. You can get into this zone when driving fast, and seem to know what is happening up ahead. You can get into it when studying with the radio on instead of trying to force your concentration. You can easily get into it when doing something rhythmic like drumming or long distance running.

The strand allowing us to create our own versions of reality is of course affected by our experiences all along the way. We tend to think that things happen because of cause and effect, and they do, but they can also start to happen as you direct them once you become aware that you can change your reactions. It's very simple really, I mean if someone is horrid to you there is just no need to be horrid back, if you laugh gently and just let it go for example instead, knowing you aren't going to let it mess up your day, then it will be more likely to change the other's outlook too, than if you had responded in kind. Then maybe you can remain friends and take the chance some other day to do something interesting together.

Back to the relationship thing again, and communication - **All relationships are reflecting your relationship with yourself.** If you keep showing the good strands of you instead of the ego reactionary ones, then you will respect and love yourself for it. If you do that for others too your relationships will soar. I mean if you tell a guy every day how badly he does something then he is pretty soon going to turn sour, but if instead you focus on telling him about the good things he does, then he will blossom and you can get on a lot better. It's the same with things in your day too, if you focus on the good things like that the sun is shining and you are going to see your kid that evening, instead of complaining about the work you have to do, then pretty soon you will notice that you are enjoying life a bit more, and you notice other things big and small that make our world beautiful. It really is as simple as that.

Of course love, respect, trust, and honesty has to go both ways in a relationship, you can't have one party taking advantage of another, so good communication is also needed to stand up for yourself to ensure this balance. Ideally all relationships, including friendships, should be about supporting each other to be the best they can be and live fulfilled lives. Again, although we are all amazing individuals with diverse ideas, skills, and needs, we are also part of various teams – family team, work team, friendship team, humanity team.

I have trained as a counsellor and life coach, so this helps my understanding of our relationships with each other and with what we want to achieve in our lives. I have always noted a great difference in two strands of therapy, in that there is one that mulls over & over problems, holding onto clients for as long as they can so that they can earn their money and validate themselves, and there is the other which I am glad to say I have always belonged to, that enables clients to take control as soon as possible. We enable them, we give them tools, we let them bounce off us, but they find their own ultimate answers with our solid support and gentle guidance.

Brief Solution Focused Therapy takes people straight away from the focus on their problems to focus on their strengths. No matter what a person presents with there is something they have managed to do to get themselves to come along, to make a choice about this situation, so that is a great starting point, and once they start looking at how far they have already come they can soon see that they are going to be able to go on from there instead of feeling hopeless about the unmentionable P (problem) word.

In all these areas, it only takes one small swing from the negative to the positive to start making a big difference. Positive progress goes in amazing leaps, just like evolution has done, (but we mustn't forget to reassure people that if they do lapse a little, that is perfectly normal, they just need to get back on track and not get disheartened. We tend to expect very highly of ourselves, which is good, but it really does not pay to beat ourselves up for the odd lapse). A therapist who works in this way feels validated at a much deeper level than a therapist who tries to hang on to her clients so that they can go on talking the endless talk instead of getting them out there to start walking.

Okay, so, this stream of consciousness which is now rather fragmented into various strands, needs to be kept an eye on. If we aren't too careful we can soon lose track completely of which strand is the real one, the deep grounded one inside of you. If we start to think that the reality we are creating is real, then we can get sucked deeper into that by creating more and more strands in that area and tying ourselves in knots. People can become totally money conscious, thinking everything depends on that, when really that is just part of a strand we created to enable us to trade within the strand that is logical to our egos. The idea of possession makes the ego feel good, and it tries to collect more of whatever works for it…. For some people that might be sexual possession, or it might mean fame (audience possession), or it might be addiction because that is the only way they feel they can get enough of this particular physical strand aimed at gratifying the ego, which usually ends up numbing the other parts of us. If our egos feel threatened they will try to build up power in whatever way they can to protect themselves, but actually true power comes from knowing that the ego is not needed for all levels of our lives, that we have other parts of ourselves that we can depend on. Our poor little egos can be easily frightened by the news, especially as it concentrates on the negative stuff, but the deep strand of consciousness within us can take us outside of that and keep faith and hope alive.

Of course you need the ego to continue in this world, you do not destroy it, *you just relax it so that it does not run away with you.* You can still be an individual and do remarkable things with humility. Your character does not depend on your ego. The ego is just the attention seeker, control freak part of you – often motivated by fear of losing something, (which is a crazy unbalanced fear, as acting from ego makes us more likely to behave in ways that wind up with us losing the very things we think we need, than if we acted with humility). If you let ego lead, you try to hold onto people who you think fill gaps in your life instead of being whole in yourself first and then finding the right people to be with (as there is then no imbalance). If we are ego led we have tantrums when we think someone is behaving at odds with our perceived needs, instead of talking rationally with them to explain what it is you think you need. Humility is strength. *Lots of things that the ego tries to tell you are weak, are actually strong,* that is why the ego fears them.

With the ego subdued, a guru may be able to maintain a balanced state most of the time, but the world and life around him continues in a flux. There would be little point in sitting in a permanent state of meditation though, as it would be like opting out of the experience of living fully, like not really being here. So we have to surely integrate our highest levels into the 'real' world with all its contrasts – learn to live in balance with all parts of ourselves, including a healthy ego - and it must be our response to this 'real' world that counts.

In order for us to appreciate the possibilities of life we need to, physically and mentally, experience contrasting levels (everything between 'healthy' and 'unwell', 'angry people' and 'relaxed people', 'love' and 'fear', for example). If everything was in a constant state of sameness (no grades of 'bad', 'good', 'better', 'best'), then existence would hold no meaning for us, and we would have no impulse to strive towards anything. Without the apparently opposing states of being 'alive' or 'dead', how would we define life at all. So we have to have these contrasts - to enable us to exist, and experience the variations available to us, and thus enable us to evolve, whether consciously / positively or not.

(Evolution doesn't have to be positive does it, it just involves making adaptations; and evolving consciously doesn't have to be positive either does it, it all depends on your intention. We have constant choices about what to do with our awareness, and what possibilities to follow. Higher consciousness usually entails a blissful sense that everything is interconnected and therefore we strive for balance & the good of all, not just people, but all living things, ecosystems, and even the planet. It also works through love; whereas lower, ego based consciousness focuses on the self, and is happy to evoke chaos in order to win power & privileges, working through fear of threat to that self. Either 'side' can deliberately train their minds to overcome both emotional & physical obstacles, and achieve what they wish. Greed must be like an addiction of the ego, with self-revulsion submerged in it's pursuit in a similar way to with other addictions. However, a lot has to do with family lineage / example, and active encouragement of that pursuit, so fear of change is even stronger.

However, change from ego based power towards power of higher self is always positive.)

We may start off with taught experience, or patterns handed down to us, but soon we can begin to learn from our own experience, and constantly assess our decisions of what to do, and how to represent ourselves in the world, in the light of this. If we don't experience the darkness then we can't understand light, our sense of good is coloured by our sense of evil. The list of paradoxes goes on, and we will look at several later, but really **all paradoxes are just two separating strands originating from the same source….. you can't have one half without the other for they are part of each other.** Empty/full, hungry/replete…. all obvious things, created by our need to exist in a physical world. As long as we have some sort of an awareness of the spiritual strand, then we will keep some perspective on this, but we can so easily get lost. We can become mightily confused and get drawn into all sorts of myths and dramas, and manifest so many things against each other, instead of returning to the unity of the stream. (I am not saying myths are bad, there are many good stories we can tell ourselves to explain the levels of understanding we are at, and help us cope with life at that level, but we should recognise them as parables and move on to new levels with new stories that work for us, until again we rewrite these.)

Even if you don't think there is any purpose to your existence, beyond us being here and experiencing life on this planet, we still need these apparent paradoxes to enable us to exist here at all. The paradoxes create a frame or span or network where otherwise there would be no place for us to exist consciously in any individual form. We could not separate out from the original stream of pure consciousness or energy. "I think, therefore I am" could be expressed conversely – If you have no frame of reference in which to think, then you cannot BE conscious of any sort of YOU.

The soul is like a template to guide us, with frequencies of light and sound linked in to our physical bodies. The heart, being at our centres, is a more reliable base to work from than our brains, and we can in fact master our minds and train them to always work for us instead of against us as they sometimes do. We know in our heart of hearts, the core of our being, who we really are, and how we should live. It's just that we get caught up in our busy minds, and distracted from that, until we even forget it is there. I think it is fine that we have used our minds for so many things, but focusing on that area so much has also been very destructive, and we have allowed ourselves to be led astray by others who wish to control us and plunder the planet. It is time to return to the heart, and use our minds in a more heart-centred way to create better ways of living, personally and globally. We can then use our minds to create what we truly need, instead of making all these false starts, and sabotaging ourselves.

If you have been seeking in the spiritual arena then you are lucky, for the deep running strand in you will keep helping you, it won't just abandon you once it knows that you want to understand at some level. But be aware, as it can sometimes pull you back quite sharply when you don't heed it. Think of it this way – if you set out to climb a mountain, then in the low valleys where there are many wandering paths, it does not matter which one you take too much. You will find out a lot of things and hopefully enjoy yourself along the way, developing all your senses and becoming physically fit - and perhaps never falling too far (a little slip here and there actually teaches you more, so you become wiser as you journey on). But if you have done all that and are ready to aim for one of the high peaks, then you need to be more focused, so once your intention is set, your spiritual strand is with you every step of the way and if you start digressing, it literally forces you to face back the right way, even if it means getting sick so that you have to stop and think about where you are going, and find your balance again. It doesn't want you to fall off a cliff you see!

That is what happened to me. I had just got to the point I knew I would one day get to, where I could see things clearly enough to write this book….. and yet the final few steps had been so small and inevitable, that I almost missed that point. I could have gone back to work, carried on seeing my clients one by one, carried on partying and playing saxophone like a wild thing, and not realised that this time had truly come. So I got sick so that I had to lie in bed for several days and hallucinate, and in the less delirious stages, I had a series of epiphanies where I saw that my life was now completely changed. I needed to make this book my main focus and all other things would fall into place. I could see many small details too, how certain people fitted into my life in different ways to what I had thought, and what certain things from the past meant, etc. I continue to go on learning – it really never stops. There is so much information out there, ah but what is real and what is not?

Of course, this book is only my view of things, but I have been so dedicated to learning through wide experience, and study, that I do feel it is worth sharing – to help others who are seeking ways of looking at things that might be helpful on their own journeys. I think my ideas make it so much easier to step outside the limits we tend to find ourselves in. This gives us the freedom and awareness to become beings of grace, tuned into the full potential of life.

Interestingly, even if you don't believe my theories, looking at things from this perspective will still have the effect of making you more aware of things you can rise above and beyond if you wish.

I think that you will find the book unique. There are a lot of similar ideas about spiritual or personal development out there, but I think that my views contain something more in both their detail and their entirety. I hope the overall perspective is helpful.

I make no apology for including all sorts of different types of writing, plus the graphics, in one book, as we interpret (and celebrate) the world in a multitude of ways. For me the different forms add together to convey fuller meaning, precisely *because* of the different kinds of expression they allow.

Please take the book with love, and go out and live a life of choice in a world I hope you will no longer see as quite so chaotic!

A View from Outside the Matrix -
that allows the 'normal' world to exist.

A web of apparent paradoxes seemingly creates chaos through our emotional responses to them, but allows us to experience the widest possible range / variety of feelings. As we become more conscious of what we are doing, we can evolve in more self-directed ways rather than in random and confusing ways.

Without this matrix of apparent contrasts or paradoxes, we couldn't really exist as individuals. If we were physically alive at all, then life would be much the same for all, and there would be no real purpose in us having separated out from the one original consciousness into individuals.

Once you realize that this matrix is really an illusion – in the sense that it is not the defining span of reality itself, but a limited construct to allow a variety of experiences to happen - you can then learn to step outside of it, to be **objective** instead of subjected to its apparent vagaries. You still live in it at the same time of course, although in a much more conscious way than before. (It is the difference between being carried away, terrified and helpless, in a flooded river - and learning to use a canoe to direct exactly where you are going so that you maximize the fun and exhilaration the current provides and at the same time achieve a desired result.)

Not only do you set yourself free, you also become more aware of your link to the infinite stream of consciousness (or life force) all around you everywhere and in everything. This helps you navigate, and then purposely create your own life and choose who you are BEING.

Living with part of your awareness reaching 'outside' the confusion of the matrix, allows you complete choice in every moment of every day. Instead of being pulled around like a puppet on a string, or in a strong wind, dancing to everyone else's unconscious tunes, sidestepping and jumping through hoops; you become strong and steady and are able to direct your life purposefully.

Your personal (non-egocentric) power is magnified even further if you are able to remain centred in the feeling of love that your connection with the ultimate stream of consciousness will bring you. Egocentric people tend to lose their way in another sense, losing the pure joy at the heart of existence because they have misinterpreted where power should lie – it should be in the heart not the ego – and it does not come from the artificial things that the ego looks for.

If you can get your clouded, buzzing mind out of the way, at least some of the time, and stop reacting randomly to every little thing, then you can start to step free from the trance, gain more clarity, and make your own decisions about how to go on, blissfully becoming more conscious of your choices.

You still live in the old world, experiencing physical experiences, but you largely direct what those experiences are. Even those you don't direct exactly, you at least direct your responses to, so that you get the best out of them, even if it's learning a lesson the hard way.

You know there is a lot more outside of that too, and you begin to experience things that would normally have been outside of your realms. You widen your world to view a much bigger picture of it and yourself.

The dream of life twists and turns, / It could take any path, / But when you wake, you take control, / and laugh in joy at the teasing world!

Life in the matrix (like the ride of the canoeist) becomes more vital because you see that it is meaningful to celebrate experience, to be awake to the diversity of life, and indeed to be creative with your life.

I become a living paradox, wild yet calm, and many other supposed opposites which in truth are all one, neither introvert nor extrovert, but a bit of each, I like to taste many things, to discover which I wish to keep.

Reality is not the limited views we each construct, different for everyone, but a combination of everything inside all of us here, and everywhere, and underneath the surface it runs like a clear stream across multi-verses and beyond all concepts of time and space. We are joined in consciousness whether we realise it or not, all of us, and everything else. What a way to be at peace!

There is a delicate balance between creation and destruction, but even what is destroyed is used in re-creation. Everyone and everything can be transformed. Hydrogen and Oxygen, two dry gases, combine to make water! Every chemical bond produces an emergent (new) property. Sodium and Chlorine – two poisons – make salt. The sugar extracted from food fuels new thought. Planets explode and new ones coalesce. Black holes suck in matter but also spew stuff out.

In my visions I feel an umbilical suck and pull between universes, I feel layers and layers of dimensions, I feel comforted yet also exhilarated by it all.

Clarity of awareness, which is full knowingness (not just beliefs), comes from feeling the wonder and wholeness of life. If you experience this wonder and wholeness then you stop fearing the loss of material things, you become non-attached to the sort of results your ego would have wanted, and think purely in terms of what is best for the whole situation. So you don't care if someone points out that you might have slipped up for example, because you are ready to say, okay maybe I did and I'm sorry, but now I know different let's work to put it right. There is no sense at all any more of not wanting to lose face against each other, for there is no other, there is only the whole. There is no one to blame and no one to forgive, these things become superfluous once you step away from the idea of being only separate and needing to defend that, into the idea of the whole stream. You can feel free to ask for help though, for everyone is an aspect of this whole.

What have been called
PARADOXES
are never what they seem.
If you look deeply into them
They merge
to show us that
all the world
is really ONE.

Of course, we need to be separate *and* interconnected, not just one or the other. We are still individuals going about our lives, but with a much wider perspective, and with more stable functionality. We have to first be individuals anyway, in order to appreciate and experience the wholeness. Then we can turn our skills to working with our various teams - our friends and family, our local communities, and the rest of the world. We can always continue to learn, evolve, and have fun.

To look at SOME SUPPOSED PARADOXES

Individual identity & uniqueness Vs Community & group belonging.

As we have seen, we are single individuals, with unique characteristics, often spending time alone, yet we are part of a community – of humankind – but beyond that – part of all the stuff of the universe – belonging with all of creation.

We always have responsibilities for our own existence, thoughts, actions – but we also have responsibility towards our fellow beings and towards the continuing existence of all around us. If we are evolving, surely the only way is through harmony with all.

I believe that a lot of our confusion is due to a feeling of having lost any sense of connection with the wider community, and with the rest of creation. Families are so much more split up, moving around with jobs so less likely to have extended family support nearby, both parents working, struggling to survive financially, less time to spend talking or doing spiritually connecting things like having walks in nature, and a lot less quality time with the children.

What does it mean these days to be part of a nation? Is there anything at all to be proud of? How do we get to discuss our feelings, opinions, concerns, ask questions? Systems of education, capitalism, economics etc seems to beat individual thought out of us. We are expected to fit into boxes, watch things on boxes, work, comply, shut up, pay taxes, and buy.

I run workshops to help young people called **Transitions into Adulthood** aimed to help address this, and to teach a variety of skills for a meaningful life.

Separateness / Oneness

So, continuing from above, we are apparently separate physical beings, yet we know we are connected with all. Whether we like it or not that is the case. We need to learn to like it as everything we do affects everything around us, and thus ultimately also affects ourselves, so the only way forward is in harmony. Surely it is better to be part of a harmonious whole than to try to exist as completely separate entities.

Mind / Actuality

As we have seen, our minds too often get in the way of harmonious blending with the flow of the universe. We think complicated things that tie us in knots of emotion and confusion, when really it is simple clarity we need. If we learn to use our minds appropriately, to help us rather than hinder us, then we will find life much easier.

People all have different views of what is real according to their personal paradigms, but in actuality we are all connected, so each view is part of the whole, but the actuality of the whole is a simple truth, stripped of all the confused ideas of the masses.

I don't suppose any of us really know what reality is even if we try to look at it with scientific detail – our views are all subjective according to how we are looking at it. However, in each of our own minds, when we meditate well, we can access a mystical vision. We can sense the beautiful serene completeness of creative energy that communicates to us how a whole amazingly diverse universe can simply have been created and continue to evolve.

Everything has to be part of it. There can be no actual boundaries, separations, or paradoxes. Anything like that can only possibly ever be explained as some construct, whether of our minds or otherwise) that makes it easier for us to deal with life until we can become aware enough to see beyond its limitations.

Particles / Waves

We used to think these were two different things but quantum physics shows us that things at fundamental levels exist as both, depending on how they are observed.

We know that both matter and antimatter exist. We know that the earth has poles like magnets. We know that there even seems to be a pattern to systems that first appear chaotic. We know now that there are probably several other dimensions apart from those we commonly apprehend.

Perhaps Quantum Physics has come to the fore only now that our consciousness is able to begin to grasp its concepts. In the past, many scientists have gained knowledge from a dream or vision that has helped them solve a problem, so the mystical can fit together very usefully with the scientific.

Information Pathways & Communication

Information in altered states of consciousness is much more conceptual or symbolic than logical, but there is certainly plenty of it. When you empty your mind to make room for all of this, then it becomes filled with rich knowledge, which is different from learned knowledge in that your whole being seems to know it in an intuitive way. Things that seemed out of reach become intimated. Visions unfold mystically and time becomes like beautiful warm sand.

The heart and all the major organs, including the gut, are now understood to be wrapped with neurones (i.e. brain material), therefore our awareness is not limited to our heads or intellect – so gut instinct, and heart centred-ness, really do mean just that. We have many ways of receiving, processing, and transmitting information.

The development of the Internet has added to our ability to Consciously Evolve. It is such a wonderful tool to enable us to access vast quantities of information! The more information we have, the more we can choose how to be in this world. Even music recording systems allowing one person to do all their own tracks, makes music exactly as they mean to put it across. The same with book publishing, and film has developed so that it is easier for smaller groups to put together deeply spiritual or philosophical films. Anyone can make videos with minimal resources. We can easily & speedily sign petitions & support causes.

Other Media has opened up a lot too and it is easy for anyone to take a good long look into various areas previously closed to us, but news releases are still very controlled. There is still a blockage in the collective throat chakra (communication) of the human race (whether we view the responsibility for that as being outside of us or not), but we may be getting somewhere. Until we can all speak totally freely, and be listened to, against national and international manipulation, how can we truly speak up for rights, peace, and our environment?

This is where I believe we need most to evolve right now. In communication, and in all our relationships with each other, there is so much to learn. While we have developed our ability to receive and process vast amounts information in such a variety of ways, we lag far behind in our ability to actually communicate maturely and effectively with each other on personal as well as community, and international levels.

Emptiness/Fullness & Far/Near & Past or Future vs Present

When you empty your mind, it then becomes more filled than it has ever been. The whole universe seems to live inside you when you switch off your surface awareness of the things about you and your rushing thoughts – to be STILL.

When skilled at meditating, you can literally empty your mind of things connected with the 'ordinary' reality around you which normally occupies your mind so much, often going round in useless circles, tiring itself out, wasting time, trying to resolve issues but getting nowhere.

If you empty your mind of all this you can then make space for your mind to connect with the wider universe – the intelligence in the spaces between atoms. This can bring you great visions, solutions, effortless answers, peace, magnanimity. You can just let it happen and recall afterwards if there were lessons in your experience, or if it was just an 'experience', or you can learn to use it for all sorts of purposes.

In healing, for example, you are in a meditative state and yet you focus. You can see and feel things going on inside your patients' bodies. You can adjust the flow of energy and untangle blockages. You can calm hot spots and feed cold ones until they come back to proper function. You can also call on help from the 'outer edges' of perception.

There is no actual distance – what feels initially distant comes closer and more into focus. Or what is no longer needed, recedes.

There is not actual time – we sense our original perfection overlaying the now and we can use our intentions to merge them, thus making a better future.

Merging logical & 'non-logical', 'normal' & 'altered' states, focus & detachment

In this age I believe we can do with our minds alone what shamans used drugs for. We can alter our states of consciousness willingly, without the need to trick our minds with hallucinogens. This makes it far easier for us to maintain 'control' and direct our experience – so that we can use our altered states with some logical precision while at the same time benefit from being in a 'non-logical' reality (where we can accept and use what we perceive, yet at the same time marvel at its wondrous nature).

One can experience many 'levels' or 'planes' simultaneously, and the sense of detail in each is amazing, sitting parallel with the overall concept of being. If there were only 2 levels, we could use an analogy of a child observing the myriad insects under a rock whilst also feeling the shadow of the bird hovering overhead.

When we are making changes in a very constant way, we can achieve magnificent results – but a healer needs to learn much about doing things the way the patient wants them done – and not allow his own will, or that of others, to impose. The intention always needs to be for the best possible result as far as the patient is concerned. For some that may even be to find the peace to let go of this world this time round rather than to recover. In this case, although a healer may see a potential way of recovery, they will also know at a deeper level that the patient will resist this. For others it may be to learn a lesson from their situation before they can let go of the condition and recover. A healer may be given clues about this, so may try to coax a patient in the right direction, but it's best here to let things go at the pace the patient wants rather than push too hard. If you do push it, you risk losing their trust and thus cannot be of any further help, ever. We cannot expect to just heal everything every time, even though we often do get instantaneous results. There is a natural process of life that we cannot stop – we can only improve or enhance being – we cannot force nature to arrest its natural cycles.

To move away from the healer / patient analogy to a larger one, where each of us communes in our individual ways with the wider universe: When we manage to place ourselves on the paths we feel the most imperative to follow, start doing what we feel drawn to, or to put it another way, doing what we were 'made' for, this may not necessarily seem logical to others, or even to us at first, but we just know we have to do it, and trust that things will become clear.

We can do some pretty fantastic things with the right intention. We can practically start our lives over, change direction, re-train, move elsewhere, follow whatever dreams we may have.

The experience of living and functioning in 'the flow' or in a heightened state of consciousness is extraordinary, and yet it has become more 'ordinary' in the sense that it seems more readily available to us now. I think that perhaps the consciousness around us has evolved to allow this. If one thinks of collective consciousness as including some record of all past experience then it makes sense that such experiences would become more readily available to us. There is no question nowadays that there are different 'levels' of reality all somehow existing alongside or even within each other. Patterns in our wider universe seem to reflect patterns within our atoms. There are resonances and reflections everywhere. Fractal patterns in our lungs and brains look the same as those in plants, and in star systems.

We can always look to nature to better understand physical functionality and ourselves, yet we sometimes forget that we are part of nature, and tend to treat it as something separate from ourselves. In enhanced states of consciousness however, all is knowable, though it is often difficult to record and understand all this often highly conceptual and symbolic information, just as it is difficult to remember exactly how one got from point A to B when in a drug-induced trance-like state. The memory is extremely fallible, and in any case, each person will likely experience their state differently. There is no discrepancy here - whether it is an 'altered' state or a 'normal' state, we all experience things differently simply because we are all different physiologically and psychologically. We have had a whole range of different experiences affecting us as we have grown up, and these will colour our views and behaviours so that we will interpret things differently and react differently, thus again changing the next phases even further from those experiences of our fellows. Certain people may react strongly to certain sets of circumstances for example although others would not be fazed by those same conditions.

A person who is unconditionally loving for example, should remain loving whatever s/he faces. If they are aware and objective enough to avoid trigger reactions which would trip them up – mostly by stopping to think about viewing the circumstances differently than they would have previously – then they should consciously maintain that loving state, and respond (rather than react) in a loving way. Of course, none of us *are* constantly in this state, but we can try our best, and we can make amends when we realise we have slipped up.

You will always be tested if you declare yourself to have mastered a state – so allow for this! If you say you are something, then the intelligent universe asks you to prove it by being that, whatever it might throw at you. Only then would you truly know for yourself that you are what you say. Similarly, if you decide to focus on something, the universe will seem to throw distractions at you to test that you truly mean it. We just have to set these distractions aside and return to the path, and the more conscious we are about this happening, the quicker we will be able to return. You learn to re-affirm yourself, who you are being, and what you are doing. So, as we follow our path, whether it is to be a loving being, or to follow a career with a view to exploring and sharing knowledge, or whether it be both, and more besides (such as having a lot of fun), we will do this best if we retain a sense of clarity about what it is that we are aiming to do, and remind ourselves regularly of this – sort of doing a route check to see that we have not lost our way. You become yourself gradually by practicing being more and more of that and not deviating much.

Life is very full of other people and other forms of life all being who they are. Some are not very conscious of who they are being in some parts of their lives, but try not to judge them, they are still being who they are at that time, and there is nothing wrong with that at all. People usually only seek to change if they themselves perceive a need for it. The trick is not to be distracted by all that, to be a little detached and yet at the same time notice what is meaningful to you.

When you help others you still need to remain detached rather than get drawn into their reality, or you can lose sight of the bigger picture, and start becoming attached to certain outcomes. Detachment means that you can offer help with the intention of it being the right help for that person, without expecting any preconceived result.

Your main responsibility is to keep your own conscious journey as your number one priority. If you do not focus on first of all being yourself then you become lost, a misrepresentation of yourself. You then start making misrepresentations all over the place, so it is irresponsible to not be yourself. If you cannot be your own truth in the world then you have gone backwards instead of forwards….. but do not worry – worry is a waste of energy – just wake up and return to your path. Time is irrelevant really – you will get another chance – but it might as well be now – this day, this dawn, that you just say "okay, let's take another step in the right direction, even if only a small one."

It is all like meditation. When you start, you have to put distractions aside, and gently, gently relax the mind. When you are walking your own path, you find things easier because you have set other things aside – life opens up to you in all its wholeness. Once your intentions are defined with clarity, things seem to slot into place!

Obviously you still have to deal with things like paying bills etc, but you can deal with them efficiently, then lay them aside again, just like intruding thoughts, and get on with the main thing of living your life in the way that you choose, consciously. Or you could deal with them mindfully, making it a positive experience, perhaps giving thanks for the services or facilities that have become available to you, in the same way as we might give thanks for the matrix that allows our individual existence & experiences in the first place.

Is Divine Ecstasy better than drug induced ecstasy?

Yes – what comes from within is always powerful! The bliss within conquers all external influences. What may have been perceived as a threat simply no longer is. Latch onto the power in your heart-mind, and learn tools to help you use it to choose how you want to exist. It's all free too, and doesn't have any side effects!

Forget your habits of the past and journey freely into the unknown. (If you have used drugs before then you have subjected your body and mind already to the unknown, so you should not have any more to fear by trying this path.) You are here to create and experience the fullness of what is possible. There is such wonderful variety to celebrate.

Surrender, love, open, appreciate the richness, accept. Let your soul prance naked with the leaves in the wind. Let your love flow like the love of painters painting, or musicians playing, or dancers dancing, freely, expressing.

But even here, both can be part of the same thing. If you desire to try out certain experiences as part of your journey, your exploration of consciousness, then I would suggest that you are probably going to learn something interesting.

'God' Power / Human Will

I am not religious at all, but I speak sometimes of 'God' simply to include something for those who are. I don't see any reason to believe that our beliefs should separate us, surely they can all be part of the same thing, just like all the other things we usually see as paradoxical. Each one of us searching for answers could find their own belief systems equally fitting, but one is often limited by beliefs, whereas surely we should try to be all inclusive, and think beyond such systems?

So, surrendering your ego to 'God's' power does seem to connect you to 'Him' if that is what you believe in, but if you see him as some other being, a punisher if you do not do his will, then you are creating separation from 'Him'. 'God's' power is surely love and that love is within us all. The human will or ego can be surrendered just as easily to that love within, which makes you so like 'God' you are then at one with 'Him'. 'He' lives within you then in every moment, 'He' still leaves you free to follow your own will but you will find that your will becomes aligned with 'His' anyway.... Not that he is trying to impose anything on you, just that his creative life force can help you to be who you really are meant to be. The 'God' power can obviously be whatever you want it to be – the universe, or source, by any name.

Surrender does not mean that you do nothing or lose control. It means that you relax to become part of the greater flow, and are thus able to work with it, use currents in that flow to go where you want to, instead of trying to fight against the stream.

Surrender / Responsibility

Surrendering can actually make you more responsible, as once you realize you can work WITH the stream instead of fighting against it, you can achieve much more, and your plans make better sense, plus you tend to be more motivated to get on with them.

Surrendering your ego stops it from getting in your own way as well as preventing it from trying to trip up other people, thus once again, you are more responsible.

Invincibility / Vulnerability

Two sides of the same coin - at one time we could feel one way and at another time another... so we can be both, or we can be neither once we have mastered these concepts - that allows the ego to relax its fearful jaws.

Steady Vs Unsteady / Emotionally Vulnerable Vs Strong

Lots of the stuff in this book will be giving you inspiration I hope, to help settle these ones out.

If we are evolving we learn to be steady instead of unsteady, so that we don't just react blindly and emotionally to things, but step back to consider them from a proper perspective. This also means that we are becoming more emotionally strong and leaving behind some of our vulnerabilities, yet we accept some as being inherently human. Seeing the bigger perspective on life helps us to feel more secure, more centred in ourselves, more able to find our way in life and thus more able to do things the way we want to, free to make our own choices.

Love / Hate & Anger / Fear

All these emotions can be dissolved by the first one, love. That is all there is in the end. When you love thy neighbours, and all strangers, then you love so much you can never have enemies, the word enemy becomes superfluous, as does the word forgiveness (for there is nothing to forgive). When you love so much there is no hate. When you love so much there is no more anger, just curiosity to learn why things needed to happen that way. When you love life and understand that the source is never ending, then you know that there is nothing to fear, for all is just a journey of experience. And each person acts according to their experience, and other knowledge gathered, so they cannot suddenly be expected to leap beyond that without some sort of help. We should try to understand the other's position, and help them to understand ours, by communicating respectfully, and not fly into careless anger which only hurts everybody. It is often fear of losing control of our neat little worlds that causes us to react, but people and lives do not fit into boxes, and we should allow them to be free to be who they choose to be. We can all adapt, and appreciate diversity.

Through Pain and Hardship, to Exquisite Clarity.

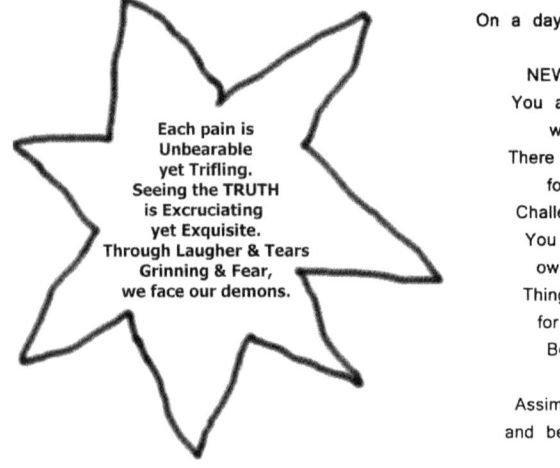

Each pain is
Unbearable
yet Trifling.
Seeing the TRUTH
is Excruciating
yet Exquisite.
Through Laugher & Tears
Grinning & Fear,
we face our demons.

On a day when things feel down
- TRUST -
NEW doors will open.
You are FREE to choose
what to do next.
There is room in your life
for more JOYFUL
Challenge & Abundance.
You are following your
own SACRED Path.
Things will balance out
for the better soon.
Be compassionate
with yourself.
Assimilate the experience
and be ready to move on.

You can journey mentally through imagined tunnels to get to grips with things, then come out into the light with new awareness. Poets often do this by writing, and artists through art.

Everything we face teaches us more, so though we may feel pain, we can be glad for the chance to learn more. Most things are not quite as bad as you imagined once you start dealing with them, so it's better to just get on with things than to prolong and exaggerate the pain through procrastination. Facing things is positive, whereas burying things is destructive. Rethink what motivates you.

If we are very aware we will learn faster, and perhaps need fewer lessons after a while.

Concentration / Lightness

The greatest learning happens if you concentrate lightly, enjoy learning and it will come naturally. Listening to music while you study actually works better than strict silence. Or if you are being silent, listen to the whisper of your soul while scanning the pages, and the words will seem to sing and form patterns for you.

Focus with clarity on what it is you want to achieve, then let it go off out into the universe. Do things lightly that need doing but don't let them become burdens. Put things in place but don't keep fiddling with them. Grasp an understanding of the details and step back to view the larger picture.

When you help a person, don't try to hang onto him, give him what he needs and send him lightly on his path.

Big / Small

Ideas can change Your Life / The World – no matter what size. It's relative anyway, whether we think they are bigger or smaller. Small may be more likely to grow into great. Big could easily fade & dissipate. You never know, so don't be closed off.

The little cleaning lady might make more of a meaningful difference to people's lives than the big rich games software producer. Everyone has something wonderful in them.

Very subtle changes like learning to be positive/grateful even if just for a moment each morning, can change your whole attitude, and thus your journey from there on in.

Stillness / Movement

The Japanese liked to contrast these in their haiku to show that they are inherently interlinked. In a deep river flowing there is sense of stillness too, and there is stillness in you when you breathe deeply, and stillness in the gaps between the breaths. The flow of life seems still but is full of abundance, and we are meant to experience that abundance of life as well as have periods of stillness. It is both, not either/or.

External / Internal

Nothing is really outside of you. At the centre of your consciousness everything exists, and we project the things we choose to see, the views we take up, outside of ourselves as if they were separate, but really they all come from the creative space within every one of us, which links us all to the supreme creative force.

However, our awareness is also more than our physical representation of being here on this earth. It pervades us as well as everything around us. I believe that it continues after our physical being is gone.

Life / Death - Both are just part of the same cycle

Look at nature – the clues are right there. A plant comes from a seed, grows into a plant, reproduces (flowers, fruits, seeds), and dies away, only to rise up again in the spring.

We do not need to worry, everything continues, and in any case worry never helps, so it is superfluous, a waste of energy you could use for better things.

Maybe death is even just another level of consciousness – like we wake from sleep – maybe we also wake from life into wider consciousness.

Creation / Evolution - Both are just part of the same cycle

We are spiritual beings come to experience life on earth, and our bodies and minds are tools to enable us to do so. It is up to us what sort of quality we put into the experience.

So, we are created, we evolve, we create, we evolve more. We are re-created anew, in a different time, place, and set of circumstances. We evolve further, and so on.

We don't seem to come to this world with equal starting positions. But it is often those who experience the greatest difficulties who overcome against the odds and excel and evolve the most.

They say that we come into the circumstances we will learn the most from, that it is all part of our growth, and that we come many times, until we have learnt enough. If you can believe that, it makes it easier, because you know you have another chance, that it is not the end, and that you don't have to be perfect first time! Hopefully that doesn't remove the imperative to try though!

It also makes it easier not to judge others, or have unrealistic expectations of them. They are only at the particular stage of their journey that they happen to be at this time around. Perhaps next time they will learn to love better! It's all relative.

Evil/Good, Darkness/Light , Hell/Heaven

These are just parts of our perception and not what is truly real. Without the idea of one we could not appreciate the other. Even heaven and hell are contrasts we made up according to our need for understanding. There is always light even in the darkest soul. Even in hell there must be light from the fire. Joking aside, we can literally create our own heaven or hell on earth in each moment we are here. Heaven and hell are within you, you create them according to your own choices. We can torture ourselves or we can relax enough to see clearly. We can literally walk in light.

True Spiritual 'Masters' always see the best in people. Everyone has a good side somewhere, and as an enlightened being you look for that, and do not blame them for the rest. They also always see the lessons in the more difficult experiences and therefore do not see them as "bad" experiences. They say that everyone and everything is a gift in every moment – that is why each moment is called the "present". Having this kind of faith really changes one's perspective!

Creation / Destruction

It is a delicate balance between the two, which way to tip today, never mind, we can always re-create tomorrow! Things are always created anew. The original energy cannot be destroyed, it goes on in some form or other. Yes, but it is still better surely to nurture and preserve rather than destroy, unless you truly think you can create something better?

We often treat nature as if it is some idealistic representation of beauty. It is of course a representation of beauty, but it is also "red in tooth and claw". Things grow and are eaten, whether it be plant or animal, it is all part of an unavoidable cycle, but it is a natural cycle that makes sense, that enables life to continue to happen. Nature can teach us a lot of lessons!

The difference between that and the behaviour of man is that man often demonstrates a wilful destruction that does not appreciate or respect life, or make any sense. Man, of all species, is conscious of the consequences of his actions, yet he still behaves irresponsibly in so many cases, treating things inhumanely, and wasting wantonly. He does not ensure resources he uses are replaced to ensure sustainability, and he poisons pretty much everything around him, including the soil, air, and water – and thus plants, animals, and ultimately himself, his family, and his fellows.

Of course people are also capable of creating the most beautiful things and thoughts, but even those sometimes end up being distorted or misused.

Causation / Freedom of Choice / Determinism

Although it may look as though other people throw things in our way, we can never blame them for this, it is down to us to choose what we take up and what we ignore. It is up to us to make decisions, to prioritise, and to speak honestly instead of taking on tasks that should not be ours. It is up to us to stand up and say we want things to change, to not react to someone's anger, but to say that although we love them we have to do things this way. This also means we listen before reacting. That way we can make the highest choices every time. (Of course you may not wish to use the actual word "love" if it is your boss for example, but you can behave in a warm way rather than a standoffish way, and you show that it is not personal, not *against* them, just for you to make positive moves. If you have been listening properly, usually you can make it positive for ALL.)

This is a really big one because it is the one that really gifts us a world of choice. But you should also be wary of taking too long to think before choosing what to do, lest the opportunity passes. One cannot expect one's partner (or boss) to know what you really think if you don't tell them! So remember to let people know what you would ideally like.

If other people seem to be putting things in your way then stop to take a real good look at that, because in the end only you can choose what to do with your life, how to live it.

Maybe your commitment is being tested and you just need to reaffirm your choice, or maybe you are putting blocks in your own way because you aren't ready for the responsibilities yet? Maybe you aren't clear enough, or sure enough? Sending out mixed messages to those around us, or to the universe, can cause a bit of a storm

Now / Eternity (Timelessness)

Eternity can be in the now and the now can vanish into eternity, but there is always another now, and an endless eternity, so we have plenty of time to do what we have to do, the thing is just knowing what it is that we have to do for our own lives to make them a positive part of the stream.

(I have a simple method to help find the seed of what that is within you if you are not sure.)

Objectivity Vs Subjectivity

Well, this whole book is about this really.

Everybody's view of reality is slightly different according to what sort of upbringing they have had, what beliefs have been instilled into them, what circumstances they have encountered, how they have dealt with (learnt from) those experiences, etc. If we try to remember this, then we should realise that we need to make allowances for different viewpoints, which are subjective and limited because they are immersed in certain sets of circumstances.

An example would be, when someone has done something that has hurt you – you don't just react unthinkingly, or stew bitterly about it, later telling others "look what they have done to me"; instead you try to look at the situation from their viewpoint. They might have said or done something with entirely different intent than what you initially imagine. They might have been trying to save you from what they thought would be a greater 'evil' by giving you a warning, or they may have simply been trying to be funny and have a different type of sense of humour to you, or they may have just not meant things quite that way and not been a good enough communicator to say it better, or they may simply have not even realised that might be hurtful to you as they did not stop to try to consider things from your point of view….. they may not even have the ability yet to do that.

If you are being objective, then you are able to stand back a bit from emotional distractions and subjective views and see a bigger picture, that takes account of all the various circumstances, and works out how one might wish to go forward from there.

Of course, objectivity can be useful in many ways. Some people may choose to use your circumstances or limitations against you, or treat others like pawns in a game of chess, or destroy things to gain their own ends; while others will prefer to take a fairer, more enlightened view overall, thereby learning how best to treat everyone individually and also help everyone become more effective parts of a happier team.

I hope you can learn to use objectivity to rise above the vagaries of circumstance and emotional reaction, and treat your partner, family, friends, colleagues, and even strangers, with respect and empathy.

I hope you can also apply this to yourself, so that you are able to be at peace, and have the clarity to choose exactly how you want to be and what you want to do in this life.

Embracing the Paradoxes – to Transcend them

When we come into physical bodies to experience life here, it is an involution (and a forgetting), We combine pure consciousness with a dense material/physical world, which greatly challenges us. Through our experience we can evolve upwards again.

We can use the ego, but not allow it to use us, so the denser strand is subdued as a tool to the finer strand that is the pure you.

Likewise, you have hosts of possible play acting selves you can bring out for fun, but you should never let any of them take over. So the ego is a tool, like so many other things, like the 'matrix' itself.

The world is full of lots of people play acting and hurling stuff about, unconscious of the effects. And there are large group karmic things going on through history that none of us should ever take personally. Rushing about trying to rectify the sins of the past is not productive. The best you can do is to be present as the new you in the now, holding your light as a steady candle to add to the beam of calm and love now spreading to help wake more and more people up. Hopefully we will evolve as a species to eventually cease the unnecessary conflict between different groups of ourselves.

If you can be detached from the mad swirl about you, then your soul can live happily here. To get away from the past too – detachment can help you to use memory without it using you. Though cause and effect may have seemed inescapable in the past, you *can* rise above it. You can choose to become essentially real, and thus content.

Because a 'personality' is a limited package, you need to become more than that to be able to interact with the universe. Your deep you is more real because it is connected to everything, but many of us are still unaware of this, and even if we do have some awareness of it, we keep forgetting, and get sucked back into the crazy swirl of life as we are creating it – mostly unconsciously, which is why it is so chaotic.

Use meditation or humming to connect with this deep self and let all else drift away from your awareness. Focus on the sound or breath within you. Once your mind stills, you can let your focus rest in your heart area and gently become aware of the space within that connects you to the greater space out there in the universe, and welcome an interaction between them. As the universe comes in it is like a tide filling you with joy, purifying you from any mental, emotional or physical toxins, and giving you renewed life-force. It can also give you huge insight and inspiration if your mind does not try to argue with it, but lets you just listen. (A silent intuitive conversation). The more you connect with this part of you, the easier it will become to understand the simple concepts of life, and to remain aware enough to change habits, making it possible for you to consistently choose the way you live.

So, you can see that there is no paradox really between what is out there and what is inside you – they can flow into each other! There is a gentle osmosis that connects you even when you are not meditating, once you have realized that this connection exists. It is a matter of your mind becoming open to it, instead of trying to shut it off.

Let go of yesterday and show up for yourself today with an open mind and heart. Enjoy a sensation of being ready, of being in harmony with all around you.

You are opening a channel in your awareness through which renewal, peace, harmony, love, creativity, and wholeness get a chance to be here, manifest, and support you.

The meaning of life is that **you have been given an opportunity of pure potential** in which to embrace as many of the infinite range of possibilities available as you wish. You, the observer, create your version of reality, and experience that. **Consciousness unfolds objectively in everything around us, but events inside the mind are subjective** because we all have different backgrounds and experiences, which affect the lens we look at life through.

What we experience as obstacles reflects gaps in our awareness, and we can learn to understand why, and then mend them. We can always learn from setbacks, **everything you do is about unfolding yourself to yourself.** You are the witness.

I am content to be in the magnificent flow of life, the world is in me first and then I am in it. The universe acts through our nervous systems. In every moment the world is blossoming into infinite variety, and yet falling silent to witness the amazement of its miracles. I am cared for and life is infinitely worthwhile when I can blossom and also observe enough to allow further blossoming.

When suffering or being with someone else suffering: **Do not push away those who wish to be there for you.** Hear them say - I will help you get through this – don't be afraid that you are driving me away – you are not letting me down – you can have the space you need but I won't let you be alone – I will be as real with you as I can be – I won't be afraid of you even though you may be afraid of your pain – I will do all I can to show you that life is still good and joy still possible – I won't let you hold onto your pain – we are here to get through this.

Friends are there to remind you who you truly are, and if you deviate, to help call you back. Hopefully family and partners can also be our friends in this way, loving and supporting the true you.

Letting Go:

- Make the most of every experience – go lightly
- Don't obsess over right or wrong decisions – go lightly
- Stop defending your self image – go lightly

- Make no decisions whilst in doubt – don't feel pressured – go lightly
- Grow beyond your comfort zone – go lightly
- See the positive possibilities in whatever happens – go lightly
- Find the stream of joy – go lightly!

Like attracts like – if you send the universe mixed messages about what you want to do, then it won't know how to help you. You need to present things with clarity in order to get them in the flow, so let go of confusion or you will confuse the universe about what you want. Let go of an idea while you are not clear, and return to it later.

You stop being ruled by self-image when:

You are no longer offended by things. You stop appraising how a situation makes you look. You don't exclude people you feel superior or inferior to. You *stop* feeling inferior or superior. You quit worrying about what others think about you. You no longer obsess over money, status or possessions. You no longer feel the urge to defend your opinions (though you may still wish people to hear / understand them).
    We are all really equal, but it is easy to let the illusions of superiority and inferiority creep in at the workplace for example, when you are at different levels in the hierarchy there, or in a group situation where some people are more experienced than others.
    A healer for example, does not worry about people saying it does not work, she just goes ahead and heals people. A diviner likewise does not worry about people laughing about the concept, he just goes out and finds water for those who ask him to.

Timing in relation to Communication

Timing is important in good communication. Take a moment to think for sure before answering – to avoid unthinking reactions – but don't take so long that the other person thinks there is a problem. If you need longer, then say so. Explain that you want to think something through, to give yourself time to make a truthful and thought through response – you can say you feel it is important to do so in order to be really clear, or because the issue deserves this time for full thought. Never just walk off if you can't answer at once, as that will only make the other person worry and possibly even come up with all sorts of dangerous assumptions.

But talk sooner rather than later if you do have something bugging you. Don't let it slide, as it will always be a problem again later, and probably a bigger one to deal with then as you didn't do the job first time. As soon as one starts letting things slide, they build up inside you, until one day a little thing that may seem insignificant will turn out to be the last straw that pushes you over the edge to explode with all the pent up frustration of things you have not dealt with.

Watch how you react.
Catch yourself not paying attention.
Listen to what you are actually saying.
Follow the rise and fall of energy.
Question your ego.
Immerse yourself in the spiritual.

If you think someone has let you down, look to understand the reason & find the solution rather than reacting with bitterness. They may need love just as much as you do.

Some Affirmations:

I will not misuse time through procrastination and delay (not do other things instead of what I mean to do). I will choose my path every moment of every day. I will follow my own rhythms with awareness (but not laziness). I will stop racing against the clock, and I will let go of the idea of struggle. I will nurture all parts of myself, as it is only through my own nurturing that I can be fit to do my best work, and to help others. I will always allow time to relax, have fun, and celebrate who I am being, and the ongoing journey of discovering who I will be in each next moment. I will not fear what time brings in the future. I will not regret what time brought in the past, for I have grown/sprung from it. I will let time unfold for me. I will keep in mind that there is always enough time, for it is fluid. I will trust my path is unfolding as it should - because I am in balance, clear about where I want to go, and actively engaging with my journey.

The SUFI WAY – is to experience the fullness of life

"An approach to spiritual growth encouraging both contemplative practice and the living of a full and balanced life that is present to both the joys and the sufferings of the world.

It also encompasses an ongoing search for ways to inspire change, both in individuals and the world."

"There are still wild Sufis, who are constantly tickled with life. It's scandalous how they love and laugh at any small event. People gossip about them, and that makes them deft in their cunning, but really a great God-wrestling goes on inside these wanderers, a flood of sunlight that's drunk with the whole thing…."   - RUMI

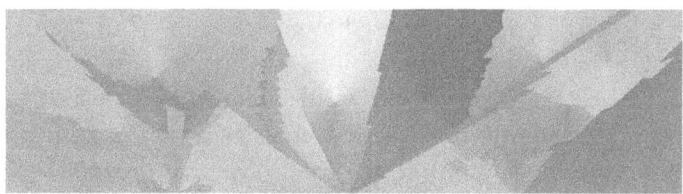

Looking back on the seeming Paradoxes stemming from Polarities

Fear & Judgement may be okay at a very practical level, as a warning to be careful of things - obviously one has to be aware of burglars maybe wanting to pick up stuff that might be left unguarded for example, just as we know not to run into the road when a big lorry is coming. We have to teach our children these things. It's just that we shouldn't get so caught up in fear & judgement that we don't see the bigger picture.

We aren't being selfish when we take care of ourselves either. We have to do that in order to do anything else effectively. If a healer, for example, just gives away their personal energy, instead of properly channelling what they use, then they drain themselves, and may not even get home safely, perhaps even hurting some other innocent party by causing an accident; so being a martyr is irresponsible, and the people you are trying to help probably wouldn't want you to be doing that anyway. A healer needs to stay grounded too. Everyone needs to balance their special skills with practicality. Just as you need to eat and sleep to function, you need to keep yourself fit and well, housed and able to pay the bills. I'm not suggesting anyone throw all caution to the wind and just expect the universe to look after you, although this can and does sometimes happen.

We do need to see all sides of things, rather than limiting ourselves to one side of a polarity or another. We need practical survival alongside a spiritual perspective, remembering that we are part of the oneness that includes (by its essential nature) huge variety. We need to accept both sides of a polarity - one cannot exist without the other. Yes, we can focus on the positive and be grateful for the good things, but we also need to be realistic and embrace the full spectrum of existence.

The same applies to past, present, and future. We can focus on the now to prevent ourselves being caught up in the past, and to stop us from putting off things we need to get on with – but again, we need to acknowledge the past is what got us to where we are (and it is still relevant, with all its lessons), and we also take steps to prepare for the future (ideally in a non-fearful, non-obsessive way). Even if life seems 'bad' right now, we can look to the past to remind ourselves of good times, and look to the future to help us plan for more. Just don't forget that today is the all important stepping stone, so make the most of it.

There are always things to discover and things to learn. Even if you think you have arrived somewhere, the journey carries on.

If you feel trapped by a situation, you can meditate on your breath, connecting you to your essential nature and to everything – and the issue will become smaller – you may even hit on an inspirational solution.

By feeling yourself as part of the oneness, it becomes easier to understand yourself and others, and to let go of situations. We set ourselves free. We feel our innocent hearts pumping blood round our amazing bodies and brains, infused with the life-force - and can truly enjoy being here.

There is NO PARADOX because, although opposite states appear to exist or be true in our world simultaneously, they are not contradictory. They are part of the same stream of consciousness which creates everything, and which makes it possible for us to experience life.

We can consciously make it our intention to experience personal specifics, then use our fuller awareness and maturing understanding to fuse our experience with ALL experience.

EXPERIENCING – Transience, Witnessing, Being

I think that part of why we are here is to experience life fully and be a witness to the vast spread of consciousness and creation. Perhaps this is so that the stream of consciousness itself can experience the extent of its own splendour through us, or perhaps not. Either way, if we live as if this is so, it enhances our lives, helping us to focus on noticing all the amazing possibilities of life. But both life and beauty are transient – the flower blooms then dies until there is another one. We cannot really capture moments from the ongoing display that continues to change before all our senses, but we can try to appreciate and reflect that wonder as it unfolds. This can enhance our relationships, our creativity, and everything we do.

Everything in this world is transient, including ourselves, and if we react in fear to that, or push the thoughts away instead of accepting this (without becoming depressed by it), then you are cutting yourself off from the ability to enjoy the beauty in each moment, the amazing experience of life itself, and all that goes with it.

It is like saying, no, I don't want to look at the flower because tomorrow it will be dead, instead of just appreciating it while you can. Surely the joy of observing that beauty, experiencing that heavenly scent, touching those miraculous velvet petals – completely compensates for the risk of allowing ourselves to engage with life rather than cut ourselves off from it?

In a relationship we need to enjoy what we have in the present moment – and that in itself is much more likely to keep it going, whereas obsessing about trying to hold onto someone, or something, or control things, completely takes away our ability to appreciate and celebrate, under which circumstances no relationship can thrive.

Once we learn to relax the obsessive mind, ideally with the help of meditation techniques, we can enjoy what we have in each moment, instead of worrying about what might happen next. We can step back from the ego attachment to fulfilling one's needs, and just appreciate the intimate connection with each other and all of life.

Yes life, love, nature, is all transient, but if we can't enjoy it while we are here then what is the point?

The material world is all an illusion, but behind that lies the timelessness where all experience is grounded and accessible, so while the flower itself is transient, the experience of connecting with its beauty is not. If we do not allow ourselves that connection then we cannot truly love others, and the world.

Do not fear it, relax into it, then you will be yourself. By being ourselves we can experience nurturing relationships where we also allow others to be themselves.

We cannot do anything about making life less transient so we may as well relax instead of worrying about it! It is the relaxation of the ego that allows the joy of intimate connection to shine through instead – what a reward! (It is a similar joy that shines through some art due to the ability of the artist, poet, etc to allow that translucence through.) So by letting go, we actually open up to new wonders of beauty and love, new heights of experience that are real and vivid. (It goes beyond any artificial high by far, and without the downer!)

As psychologist (and Buddhist) Dr Mark Epstein (New York) says - "By giving people a means of being themselves, no matter what kind of vulnerability they are bearing, meditation prepares the ground for intimacy. By teaching people how to be less self-conscious and more accepting of their own idiosyncrasies, meditation clears away some of the defensive rigidity that obscures the natural flow of love." and "It tends to work against the assumption of deficiency by restoring the capacity for connection from the inside." and "In doing this, it challenges the common assumption of our culture about where connection comes from. In the Buddhist view, connection is already present. We are not as separate and distinct as we think we are. Connection is our natural state; we just have to learn to permit it."

Perhaps it is easier for us to appreciate our connection with the natural world first, but people of course are also part of the natural world.

Multiple Witnesses / Experiencing the infinite variety of life.

In his writings on such topics as **'Oneness of Mind' & 'Mystic Vision' (as set out in "Quantum Questions – Mystical Writings of the world's greatest physicists" Edited by Ken Wilber),** Schrodinger said that what seems to be a plurality of souls is merely a series of different **aspects of the one** consciousness, produced by a deception or illusion. I like the word "aspects" as it seems to me to allow for that concept of coming from the one at the same time as allowing for us each to be individuals, with our own views and interpretations of everything we see, feel, hear……

It seems, however, that Schrodinger is saying that each one of us views or witnesses the same tree or beautiful mountainous scenery and that is all. I would argue that each of us views the tree, or landscape, differently. Each person would react differently to the same experience.

One person may love the tree because of the greenery, another because of the birds it brings. Another may want to cut it down because it blocks his view or casts a shadow on his window. Another may fear the possibility of its roots destroying his foundations. Each bird, insect, or animal present would also have a differing experience of the tree and how it relates to their lives. So the reality of the tree is multi-layered, including its biological make-up, a mini ecosystem.

It may seem that we feed back our multifaceted experiences and views to the whole, and could be why there are so many of us, all different, with different circumstances, creating different experiences, thus different reactions (as well as being different genetically). This whole could possibly then evolve from the sum of ALL our evolving experiences being fed back to it. Maybe it experiences the infinite variety of itself through us and everything else created from its original potential, directly or indirectly, and the possibilities continue to expand.

Our physical bodies and our minds are tools for experiencing the world and the interactions between others and ourselves, and we continually grow (or not) according to these experiences, until perhaps we do eventually become so enlightened, or **aligned with the divine**, that we no longer react to situations from the limited understanding of our basic ego selves, but see everything, including ourselves, as being blended with the supreme consciousness. Until then, I think we are only partly connected, and learning (as Aspects) to become ONE again.

As we learn to become more attuned to the consciousness of ONE, we become more peaceful, more joyful, more able to tap into information we can put to good use. It happens when we are in a relaxed but highly aware state of consciousness, such as driving in a lightly focused manner. One of the earliest signs is suddenly knowing that we have to slow down as something is wrong on the road ahead. We learn to go deeper with meditation and visualizations. People go on to practice therapies, to teach, and to heal. It is possible to divine for answers to any questions, as well as to find water or minerals or lost objects. We become better at these things, as with practice our awareness expands and we can stay in touch most of the time. We learn from events rather than react to them, we free ourselves of fear, we follow our dreams and allow them to unfold. We use affirmations & self-hypnosis to change embedded thinking patterns that are no longer required, and focus instead on new intentions, and eventually we create our lives much more in the way we intend. We are in control of how we respond to the world and others around us, and we know how good that feels. We are in touch with our inner selves, which are now quite obviously part of the whole. We have come home.

Let us now open our hearts and listen to what the Beings of Light can tell us:

The Beings of Light are Aspects of the Oneness too – they are a high source of 'group' energy that comes to me to channel answers to questions. They have given me many answers in my guide "Beings of Light", including details of how souls come into bodies - and also artwork, poems, songs. Their energy is fine and clear, and their messages light and conversational, even gently chiding. When communicating with them, there seems to be no difference between mind and heart, no one or the other, no distance between us, no time, only love. They are everywhere, including inside of me.

"It is all about love, when you learn to truly love the world and all creation, of which you are part, then you become one with the **cosmic mind** which is also like a heart, the way you speak of a heart (which is not like the biological mechanism, but an energy of simple and unchanging purity). You have to love yourself, for without love your body does not know how to become one whole that is optimally functioning, and you do not know how to become one with the **whole mind of life**. Love is the missing ingredient that has been so twisted by fear of what man does to the world and each other, and even to himself. If you love then you trust yourself and your others to let go of that fear which tries to hold and control you, and you become ONE. You set yourselves free to believe in the beauty within and around you and to see the infinite possibilities of creation. There is nothing left to fear because nothing can hurt you when you are whole and open. Nothing can manipulate you, you become translucent. When you are in love with the universe and all it offers, then you are on your path to becoming a creator, to making of your life what you will. Only when you love can you heal, for to heal you must become one with those you help, and bring them to the light of the cosmic mind, where there is no time, and all is knowable yet changeable."

Here is another segment of communication from these Beings of Light:

"Look inside. Every step you take in life can be a step closer to the truth inside. Every step is a choice to become more or less of who you are. Look inside and recognise the spark of who you deeply are. Look beyond the ego self. You are not a puppet that projects its mask upon this world. You are so much deeper. And the world is not the theatre it may seem to be. There is a deeper reality. Inside the body is the chance to answer all the dreams, and live the mystery with **mastery**. Inside each one of us is the energy of all creation, the knowledge and the beauty. Look inside and touch the spark within your heart. Acknowledge it with every step, and encourage it to radiate out. If everything you do in life is touched with this pure light, your being will reflect the magnificence of the infinite. Your natural presence will connect with the drifting essence of the universe, and be guided by its subtle whispers towards what is right for you in each moment. Once awake, you can consciously create the life that is your gift to make and live. Every step you take is a choice to become what you create."

As well as the Beings of Light guide, there is more about Mastery in another guide.

All of the above is extremely relevant to my theory of there being NO PARADOX in actuality. In the world we live in – yes, there appear to be paradoxes, and if there were not then we could not experience life as we know it. But in the greater reality there is one stream or beam of consciousness flowing or shining out. Each 'side' of every apparent paradox comes from the same origin. The 'opposites' are an illusion!

    It is as if a light is being shone through a glass and thus being split into the spectrum of colours. So consciousness, or life itself, seems to be split into several strands. If we didn't have these apparent opposites we could not experience the infinite variety available to us, and learn from it all. So if you can somehow manage to live in this world and yet grasp that everything blends ultimately into one, your consciousness can transcend (at least some of the time) to see the big beautiful picture of the UNITY that truly is. The more you can see this, the more you will find your whole outlook rising above the swarming mass of existence instead of getting constantly caught up in, and pulled around by it.

We understand, then we can transcend. The paradoxes are like a matrix or framework created to enable us to exist here. Once we can see beyond them, we do not discard them, but we can exist at peace.

Going back to the "Quantum Questions" book edited by Ken Wilber, the physicists all seem to agree that quantum physics does not actually have anything to do with spirituality. Ken himself suggests that we have been trying to use quantum physics to prove to people that there is a logical scientific basis to what we are saying happens in spirituality, but that this cannot be the case as it is limited to mathematics. However we do know that the observer affects the outcomes of experiments, even in biology. We also know that what we think affects our bodies, and what we do affects the whole. In the movie "What the Bleep do we know?" biochemists agree with all the other thinkers on this. In my recent nutrition course, I learnt that what we feel, think, believe & perceive (whether 'real' or imagined) affects our epigenetic systems, and this actually regulates our genes. Wow!

What all the physicists in this movie also seem to agree on is that there is a wider spiritual reality that involves mystical experiences, and that this does inform the world of thinkers, including physicists. Many of them reported having mystical visions which answered their questions or gave them a visionary opening to new discoveries.

Ken Wilber, in his introduction, shows a diagram called "The Great Chain of Being" in which there are a series of circles within circles representing domains or realms. The innermost circle represents matter & physics, the study of which is completely logical and uses mathematics as its proof. Then comes biology, which is wider as it involves the study of life itself. After that comes psychology, with its study of the mind. Then there is theology, which opens up beyond the limits of our minds & bodies to the soul. The outer circle is the world of spirit & mysticism, which permeates all the other circles. Each circle transcends but includes the ones before it. The wider circles can all inform the circles within them, but not the other way around. **Thus spirit transcends everything and includes everything – it is transcendent to the world and completely immanent in the world. It is the ground of all realms.**

Just to further elucidate, Ken says that the soul (or religious) realm includes Platonic forms, archetypes, and personal deities (including archangelic patterns). In this realm there is still some subject-object duality, where the soul apprehends Being or communes with God, but there remains an irreducible boundary between them. **In the realm of spirit though, the soul *becomes* Being in a non-dual state of radical intuition and supreme identity or gnosis. The soul and God unite in absolute spirit, with no boundaries. All paradoxes blend so that we can see they are illusory, just apparently differing parts of what is actually only one stream.**

If we didn't have these apparent opposites then we could not experience each part of the infinitely varied life available to us.... You understand each part, and then you transcend them to see the big BEAUTIFUL picture, the unity, the ground of BEING.

If we did not still live amongst these opposites then we would no longer need to be here because we would be only part of the stream again (although there may be other interim stages, as I discuss elsewhere, where we still have the individuality to review our experiences here). The fact that we can continue to live with the paradoxes, and yet see beyond them, allows us to continue to witness life on earth alongside of our newly evolving apprehension of it, so that there is more of a holistic understanding of what life can be, and of ourselves in this new state of balance.

Let us see what insight the Beings of Light can give us here:

"You are trying hard to explain what really is simple. There is a sea of life in which you swim. There is water in the sea as well as water in your bodies. There is oxygen in your bodies and in the water and in the air. That is 'God' or Universal breath which is given to you for you to take within. You cannot reject it, it is always there. You can learn to breathe optimally, and you can learn to use your life optimally, or not, and that is all. 'God' does not mind what you do, you are given the chance to become love if you choose to. It is only the emotional reactions of each life form to the rest of creation that makes it seem complicated. Interaction with Spirit itself is simple without that."

A few notes on Beauty:

Plotinus said - "Beauty is the translucence through the material phenomenon, of the eternal splendour of the 'one'."

A couple of Latin mottos stated that "The simple is the seal of the true." And that "Beauty is the splendour of truth."

Think of how music works – the ratio of harmonics. Think of how fractals repeat in nature, from the tiny to the huge.

Innate archetypes of nature (patterns of harmony, or mandalas) or symbols from the collective consciousness (CJ Jung) act as a bridge between sense perception and pure ideas. They enable a non-rational understanding, a comprehension of truth and joy in simple beauty (which transcends language barriers, as do art and music).

Think of our ambivalence towards nature, how we can both love and fear the forest for example. Think of how our psyches can twist or use perception. An old man in the woods could beat us with a stick, or he could turn out to be a wise man come to give us a meaningful message.

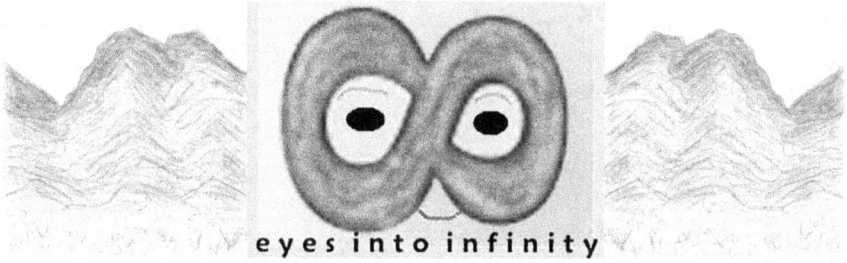

eyes into infinity

The many selves have viewed this mountain over the centuries, so the one self may know this mountain in all its multifarious perspectives.

The one self contains all the pains and joys of life the many selves have felt in each of their now's, which merge into a continual present.

Just as our eyes & brains make one image out of what we see, our many perceptions may form an overall sense of what creation is like for the ever present One, which could not otherwise comprehend beyond its own perfection.

OUT THERE

I want to be
OUT THERE -
where cool light washes
along paths beneath trees,
where babies walk on grass with bare feet,
and the dustman pauses
to eat flaky fish, or sandwiches.

I want to be
OUT THERE -
where the white collar man does not dare
to go at night time (and during the day
he is foolishly enslaved, in offices).

I want to be
OUT THERE
walking endlessly up and down those streets
that lead to nowhere new
but the music feels good, the rhythm of my feet
and the beat of the blood in my veins
so sweet and so fast
I know it will last almost forever……….

and I want to be
OUT THERE
in the sun and the rain
tempted again and again by solid old stones
with their stories of yearning.

I want to be
OUT THERE
learning the songs of rivers and streams,
recklessly riding waves of the ocean,
feeling the tug and continual weave
of currents, and winds,
ebbing and flowing.

I want to reach
OUT THERE
to touch spider thin leaves,
where birds build nests
and insects spin their own fine threads
to add to the trembling web
of the universe,
breathing.

Yes, I want to be
OUT THERE
whenever the stars beam down their tears
from away so far,
we can hardly imagine.

We could all be
OUT THERE
to catch those droplets in our hearts
and turn them into words,
for telling the world about love, and art,
as it tells us itself
over and over, every day, in so many ways.

Yes, we could all be
OUT THERE
to tell it, and each other,
about the cool light that laps and washes
along pathways beneath trees
where babies walk on grass and four leafed clovers
with podgy bare feet,
and the dustman pauses to eat.

Don't you feel the need
to be
OUT THERE
with the beat of your blood in your veins
so fast
you know it will last almost forever..........?

We could all be

OUT THERE
together, with the light
shining from our faces and our eyes
streaming down from above through our brains
and out again -
to the world that I believe in dreaming in
where I want to be
OUT THERE
gladly -
walking, laughing, loving,
praising.

Published in FIRE magazine & my book "SPIRIT SONGS"

Let's get Physical!

They say we are Spiritual Beings / come here to dwell
so that we can experience / life on the physical level.
Some are sad / thinking they are trapped
but I think it's fantastic / my body's elastic!
Some just grieve / and can't wait to leave
but I love it / I adore it / it's so GOOD to breathe!

In my physical body / I can look at your bum
and boy does it / whoops does it / turn me on!
My skin loves the stroke of your fingers,
my lips love the feel of your kisses…
They're just SO delicious!
Who'd want to miss / all this fun?

In the woods I can hug / magnificent trees
and feel the surge / of their energies.
I can watch the dances / of their branches
and listen / to the rustle of their leaves
that reminds me of streams / or salty seas
that I can taste / and smell on the breeze.

I can walk / I can swim / I can climb.
I can feel my muscles / working all the time.

I can feel my feet / on solid ground.
I can feel my blood / pumping round and round.
I can feel my lungs / going out and in,
And boy / do I enjoy / eating!

The surprise of tomatoes / bursting on my tongue
makes me feel / forever young.
The way that lettuce / crunches when you bite
makes me feel / like dynamite!
The sensation / of sucking / a strawberry
milkshake / up through a straw
makes me feel / very, very, very
much like staying here / for more.

The pleasure / I receive / every time / I give
makes me glad / to live / in this heaven / on earth
where I chose / to be birthed / to learn / to be kind
and observe / the workings / of my mind,
to enjoy tricks and jokes and games / and artistic ideas,
to let go of pain / and blast away fears,
and to try / to understand / who I really am
and what it means / to be part / of a team or a plan.

I love dancing in swirls / and twirls ….
See the shapes / I can make
as my body moves / and curls / gets into the groove.
Look at me now / I've got nothing to prove
and nothing to lose… / I do it all / out of pure love for
the extraordinary things / we can do……

So what's next? / Please don't take me away just yet…
I'd like to / have time to / experience a little more / sex!

From my book "SPIRIT SONGS"

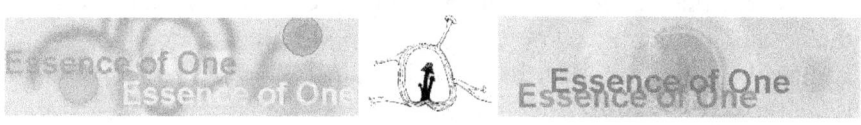

WITNESS

Witness the shape of leaves and stones, the colours created by the sun as it shines, creating a representation, a likeness of them as they are in each moment, each hour, each day, as the seasons change and the winds blow and the waters flow to reshape them or carry them away.

Witness the folds of land on the face of the earth as it turns. Witness the shadows of clouds as they march over them, bringing rain sometimes but not always. Affecting them for a time but moving on to leave them once more as they were, and yet touched perhaps gently into greenness.

Witness mist rising from the river in streamers towards the sun. Witness the grass calling to insects to come and be lovers in its thick tangled wetness. Witness the earth baring herself, for all to see her offered flesh and bones. She gives us all she has to give, and still we ask for more. Witness how we try to force her to produce miracles and expect her to go on living. Witness how we feed her poisons, and naively expect them not to get into our own systems. The rivers, the fish, the plants – all swell or curl up with false harvest we have fed them. Witness now, how we ourselves swell or curl up like foolish lovers, for we have loved the earth so well we smother her. Witness how we grow both fat and thin from what has returned to haunt us from within.

Witness the fighters in the cities where walls crumble, yet often grow again. Witness how we cannot listen anymore, for we have become used to there being so much hell, and have made hard shells to protect ourselves from madness and the tenderness of bullets. We seem too fragile to witness details fully – or we would crumble like the walls we claw against in dream-cycles where everything is futile yet quite normal.

Witness how fish leap to the hook in the brook where they are fooled by a hand-tied fly. Witness how they open their mouths to try to find the air in water they have left behind. Notice how we mouth the same replies to all that goes by in the world that we deny ourselves the ability to bear witness to. Notice how we are fooled, like the fish, by a world that reflects a dimmer semblance of reality than the reality that exists, hidden unacknowledged, deep within. Notice how we are high and dry in a tide that has turned against what we had learned and hoped it should be. Witness how we yearn for that which we dreamed of in our youth so gleefully. Witness how we flounder in our lack of freedom to be who we know we could be. Witness how we are too afraid to even breathe properly.

In the stream of consciousness we gasp and pause as we are called to eat. Notice how our eating imprisons us instead of bringing fullness and meaning. We stumble out in the night to witness the stars as they shine in the darkness, symbols to us of some hidden or unreachable dreaming. Then we have another drink. We long to witness other worlds when really we would exploit and destroy them. The stars seem to beckon and call us towards them, yet if we flew in unprotected, they would bite us back, burning or freezing or poisoning us before we poisoned them.

Witness the moon as she glows to love us and haunt us at the same time, and notice our ambiguousness. We are not witnesses steady and clear as the moonshine on waves dancing, we are unreliable and ambivalent, all with our reactions pulling us like tides of the menstrual mother back and forth in our own nightmares so that we waver and fall into the sleep of forgetting.

Awaken to the bells of the church, or cry of the cockerel, and witness the dawning. Try once more to be the one who originally answered the call by being here, by simply being here.

Witness the butterflies and lizards and chickens and dogs and donkeys all calling you to observe them, all showing you their feathers and skins, and fur and tails and wings, in the fresh light of the morning.

Witness the bridges and buildings and roads and paintings – created so lovingly by hard labour for good purpose while all you want to do is sleep again. Witness the places of worship we cling to, well and truly trawled in.

Witness the nature of water and air and fire, and how they affect each other. Witness the trees and their uses for us, and for the animals rooting in the damp heat beneath them. Witness gems glinting in dewfall, witness new snow like crystal twinkling on mountains. Witness the desert spaces where words have no reason to evolve beyond stark rocks, but simply do. Witness the shapes that nature makes in every place we turn to, to try to learn to be human in.

Witness the way we have turned blind eyes so many times to other beings, and cry inside at the emptiness we find because we have denied the details of things. We have not tried one little bit to understand, we have even lied about what we have in the dark of our hearts and grasp of our hands.

Open please, and let the light come in, help us begin to bear witness again. Stop to watch and listen to the world responding. As you learn to witness accurately, the world gives you herself more fully, and the earth breathes a sigh that may help relieve her disease, for we are each healers, or can be. When we bear witness to the truth, we enable an unfolding of harmony. When we sing to life, *we* become part of the symphony.

SMALL SIGNALS - London

This light wavering between the real and unreal,
shadows slipping through moments
that shiver past eyeballs and lips.

This kiss of time that touches us briefly
and slides away again on the breeze
or the river that yearns towards the sea.

What is the meaning of prayers muttered
by leaves in the damp streets of dawn?
What are these craven words for?

Whatever we say today will dodge away
like birds hiding in fog or thick hedges,
our forms will be tossed like dolls on the waves.

Smoke from these chimneys sends stories
of the city - upwards to dissipate
like fingers strumming strings … then nothing.

Pull on your gloves then and button your coat,
there is nothing more here for you
except perhaps stars spitting in evening dusk.

Wait… can't you even begin to say what it is
that stirs when you witness these small silent
signals of light wavering between real and unreal?

These kisses of time that touch us repeatedly,

enchant us, confuse us, wrap us up hotly. Let them go,
let their poems flutter loose like lost bank notes.

Don't wait for tomorrow for miracles to happen,
each of these signals is a miracle: time, wind, fog, damp streets,
smoke, chimneys, the river, leaves, birds, prayers....

And of course, light is the most sacred sign of all.
Right now is perfect, then gone, then instantly perfect again.
The real and the unreal interweave, are known and unknown.

What fools we are in the dance, yet what lovers
to keep wanting the world with all its stuff,
knowing in the end it will all be emptied.

What do you really want? Is there just one word
to tell it the way it is… the way the city exists
on this miraculous earth, breathing the moments out and in?

Surely there must be! Let's keep on walking
and singing, trying to find it; with these small signals
gracefully guiding us closer and closer to absolute love.

From my book "SPIRIT SONGS"

The Eternal Lover

Reach to your centre and feel it.
Reach to the heart of the earth
and feel it.
Reach out to all nature and feel it.
Reach to the master and feel it.

We are never alone -
there is always this love which pervades us,
making us One -
we have only to reach out and touch it,
or reach within.

Listen to the wind in the trees -
it feels it.
Listen to the ocean on the beach -
it knows it deeply.
Listen to the tiny insects in the sand
dunes creep.

Listen to the flowers
or the clouds,
the birds crying out,
the river calling.

There is joy of love in every corner,
every pebble,
every petal,
every feather,
every grain of sand you hold
or let go of
or envisage there before you –

Feel it in your very core,
entering every pore -
and be blessed.

Enter the world
of the eternal lover –
as the eternal lover.

You are the eternal lover.
The world is the eternal lover.
The master is the eternal lover.

Reach to the centre –
we are One.

PURELY

Loving the lives
of past, present and future —
you may smell
and may taste the obstinate breath
of existence:

Shimmering atoms
like the sound of cicadas
vibrating
and letting the light
pass through.

You may seek out —
work out the colours -
by being
a simple detailer of things
on this earth.

You may write
of the incredible audacity
of trees and pebbles
and fences and scarecrows and dirty
old windows

then point
and sing and shout out and laugh
at the way
we know and don't know in our
deafness
how to walk on.

From here
you may go to the place of silence
deep in your gut -
like melting into a universe
of gold.

From my book "BLUE BRIDGE"

SHAPE

We come to this world to experience and share, to learn from each other, with each other. No longer having to ask what life is for. It is to BE, to learn, to love, to live, perhaps to even evolve. To be with you on this earth is to be blessed!

We are one. We can interchange and shift. There are times to be like a rock. Still, with open heart and arms. Other times it is best to be like sand or a river or a flame. A hammer cannot shatter you nor a knife cut you then. Other times I am light as a feather, or a leaf from a tree on the breeze, innocent. Sometimes I fly like a bird, crying out with the joy of liberty. Sometimes I am the wind itself, absolute and complete. We can be whatever we want to be in this world. We can truly transform ourselves.

The shape of life is ever re-forming. From the day we are born, or even before, to the day we depart, we continually re-shape who we are.

Whatever you see today may look different tomorrow, changed, or even strange. We wonder what it was we saw before, or if it was something else we missed in our hazed daze, or just ignored in our glazed phased way as we tore along. We'd be stronger if we slowed right down and took a long look at what went wrong before we plundered on. We need to know how to go more perceptively yet never expect to manage perfectly. We constantly depend upon our fundamental shape for founding our relationship with the world we live in and upon, but if it's changed without our noticing, then there's no telling where we could be going. So look in the mirror once in a while to see who you are before you go the next mile. Smile at yourself in the mirror to divert the terror of being swallowed up. Really it's quite simple when you've got a grip. You can take control of your shape and make it what you dare. Once you've become aware you're part way there. Now all you have to do is wonder where you'll go from here. It's in your hands now my dears.

From my book "SACRED SELVES"

Being Here

Heart knows
My spirit is ancient
And part of the whole.

Dwelling here is confusing and lonely
If part of us forgets this
And goes searching as if something is lost.

Our systems are temporary
And make no sense
Because they are only experiments
With castles of straw
And opposites pulling us apart.

In reality there are no opposites –
Everything is interlinked,
And the dream of our world
Is not at all what it seems.
Earth is a living thing

Changing its ways, and ours,
To a more conscious vision
Where materialism and ego fall away.

I am leaf green where beams shine
To create my future
Of joining and love
Not trying to win anything,
Just being.

I am still through turmoil
Because my heart remembers
I am ancient and indestructible,
I belong
With my beautiful planet,
Though I also know more distant homes everywhere
For there is no start or finish
And there is no place apart from the rest.

I am encircled by light
And you and I are within each other.
We breathe together
Like the ocean and the wind.
There is no in-between when there is union.
There is no either / or.
There is no one or other.
There is only deep satisfaction.

My cells sing in tune with the universe
Where there is no division
And time does not run out.

Blue water and yellow sun combine
With green planet eye
And life becomes complete.

PEACE

Mist lies over the river
like the icy breath of winter angels.
Darkness gathers round... and it is beautiful.

Thank you for this life, this death,
whatever it is you are
that makes us finally see.

From my book "SPIRIT SONGS"

We are all vulnerable but do not fear this, just revel in the chance to experience that & know & grow beyond. **Sometimes it's better to show our vulnerability / pain / regrets - so that others don't think us impervious / unapproachable - be real / open.**

We celebrate beauty in life and all its possibility. In so doing, we open it up for others at the same time as for ourselves. Imagine, invent! Good dreams can be inspirations to bring in to make reality fantastic enough to share. Every moment we are new and full of infinite possibility as we are part of ALL.

Exploring Altered States - (inc Meditation, Subtle Activism, Channelling, Shamanism, Divination, etc.)

Once you start experiencing altered states of consciousness, it becomes easy to see that the reality we generally live in is very shallow and limited. You can see that it might easily be possible to create different realities, maybe just for yourself, and maybe just sometimes, or maybe for all of us all of the time, or anything in-between.

For myself, there seem to be layers that can be opened up at will. I can exist in our general shared reality, but I can step outside it into other balloons of reality too. They aren't really 'instead of', they are more like extras.

On the other hand, I do also personally reject quite a bit of the general sort of 'reality' – particularly the stuff that others try to have us believe – such as most things in the media & popular culture, which are manipulated to try to either distract us or make us conform to what others want us to think or do. History is biased according to who is telling it, and even science is biased according to what the grant givers want. Politics is powered by the sponsors who mean to get their way no matter what the party. We are told all sorts of stories about some things, and very little about other things.

It's time to make up our own minds what we accept and what we don't. Our choices colour our own reality. The more consciously we are able to perceive and consider our options, the wider and deeper our potential realities can be.

Each person creates their reality because all of their life experiences are filtered by their beliefs, values, culture, language, & upbringing. This is subtly different from other people's views of reality. If we experience something then that feeds back information to affect our reality, and our new idea of reality is a combination of the two – past and updates. Our state of awareness, and careful use of thought, can further mould that reality, enabling us to make changes wherever we want, according to our ability to follow those changes through.

Apart from becoming able to see beyond the construct of the matrix of apparent paradoxes, there are many other ways we can enhance our abilities, and help ourselves make changes. A lot of these have already been mentioned in the book, and I even shared some channelling with you early on, but we have not gone into details of the use of altered states of consciousness, or active spirituality, such as meditation, subtle activism, shamanism, divination, etc.

There is a Meditation guide available via my website, as that is used widely in many cultures and traditions, and it is a hugely effective tool for anyone to use. As I see it, **meditation should not be about retreating from life around you, it should be integrated into your everyday life as a tool to enhance your experience of it, and also to help enable you achieve many objectives.** Guided meditations can be used to help with almost anything, as well as stress relief.

We can also use meditation for subtle activism, where many people link up at the same time to send out peace etc to affect a wider situation. Experiments have shown this to work.

We can use cultural constructs such as mythological or shamanistic (imaginary) higher and lower worlds, and journey into them, or create our own (waking) dreams, in which we can find answers to help heal situations or give insight into new potentials.

With practice, I have become more able to decide on an intention prior to the journey, and to guide my experiences as I go, plus record them afterwards. However, I am always open to surprises in what I experience, which may or may not lead to new insights or understandings. My experience of any construct I use may lead me to change that construct - just as my experience of life can change my idea of what it might be about or how best to live it.

What is real? Either of these – the supposed reality – or the supposed dream journey – could be interchanged. Who is to say one is any more valid than the other? We are able to make things happen in a dream, just as we can in our waking life. Changing our daily reality is often complicated due to our limited awareness, and often involves many steps, some hardship, and some failed attempts, before returning to continue the cycle of change. If we are not very aware we may, for example, even have to resort to making ourselves ill, so that we have time to think and figure things out (become more conscious of our needs) before deciding to make some change, such as leaving a job. If we are more aware, then we can do things more smoothly. There is no reason to suppose that we cannot change our own realities simply by thinking different thoughts, just as we do in a dream. In fact the funny thing is that we might even call it "waking up to ourselves, or our situation", as if we had been living in a dream all along.

If you are able to deliberately plant seeds at a subconscious level, for example by using specific guided meditations – which you can write for yourself (I can help if you wish) – then your conscious thoughts will tend to rally around to set your new reality in motion.

The evolution of our consciousness and the evolution of the constructs we live by is inextricably interlinked.

Our awareness is the absolute key, and once aware enough, we can use our intention to lead us forward. Clarity about what we want to achieve obviously helps us set clear intentions, but it is awareness again that helps us analyse and figure out all the details along the way.

If we make changes without being particularly aware, the changes we choose may not be as helpful – for example we may know we need to end a partnership, but then we end up in another equally unsuitable one, so we have not understood the basis of our need to change, and do not really evolve our constructs or ourselves as a result of such a change. However, as we grow through experience and/or learning so that we understand why things weren't working so well, we are then able to make those changes more constructively, with some idea of what we are doing. We are more likely to make some changes to the fundamental basis upon which we make our choices.

If we are aware enough to observe ourselves experiencing our reality, including all our experiences as we go, plus our dream worlds, then we are able to learn so much from everything!

If we are objective enough to see that we are creating layers within layers, then we can learn twice as fast, and at the same time understand why we decide to make changes within these layers, and simply deciding is enough for it to be done. We do not have to rush off to see some guru – we can do this for ourselves. These days there is so much knowledge available that we can access all sorts of information to help us decide what to do, and how to do it! **This accessibility of information is part of our evolution,** and the next stage of course is for us all to be so informed that we can take the power into our own hands to achieve whatever we wish, not only for ourselves, but for the wider community, and in fact for the world.

Many of the constructs we have lived by may not have all been ours in the first place, they may have been handed to us via our family or our education, or the local community or culture. Once we realise this, we can choose to change anything just by thinking differently, and set ourselves free. It may seem initially unsafe to dissolve what we are familiar with – but when we do, it is as if we have emptied our minds of clutter (as in good meditation) and the whole universe floods in, with its endless sea of possibilities and inspiration.

This ecstatic experience of becoming one with the entire energy field is euphoric because you can ultimately know and feel everything. Your individual experience no longer counts as much, you simply are part of it – the cosmos and all its natural cycles – the intricate spiralling patterns, the infinite ebb and flow – and you can go anywhere you want, and do anything. Thus we realise that the ego is an ancient tool that used to be useful for our survival, but that can now be surrendered to a subtle background level, to allow more sophisticated methods to come to the fore – to be used to enhance our experience of existence.

We can also find out anything about an existing situation by using divination. While you sit at one seemingly normal or everyday level of consciousness, you simultaneously tap into another much wider collective consciousness, which also includes information about what is happening, or has happened, in any given place or part of the planet. You can feed back the information received to your more logical and methodical brain, and use it constructively. There is very little effort in switching between these supposedly different levels of consciousness, in fact if you try too hard it won't work, it is just a gentle sort of acceptance. Such is the change from a life of trying so hard that you always create obstacles to overcome, to a life of acceptance of being in the cosmic flow.

What is important is clarity of intention. You need to be very specific about what you are looking for and very clear about your questions, because any ambiguity can lead to misunderstood answers. So awareness is essential again. You need to know enough about what you are doing to anticipate any possible errors. One example is to be very clear whether you are asking about something now or in the past.

A shaman is always opening doors into supposedly independently existing realms, but these realms still interact with each other. They may seem like mental constructs, and the sense of their interaction may also appear to be in the mind, but they surely do affect local 'reality' (where I usually meet with you). My 'reality' could equally well be regarded as a mental construct in any case. What I think, affects these constructs in turn, so I view them ALL objectively, and use them to achieve intended results. To be able to use my intention in such a way requires an allowance that the whole host of perceived paradoxes may be dismissible, including between separation and oneness, mind and actuality, timeless journeys and the NOW.

Consciousness can flow from one to the other to and fro, like osmosis in intra-cellular exchanges. Consciousness can be in many places simultaneously, discovering visionary secrets, yet recording them, and directing them with a purpose way beyond any lucid dreaming. One can interpret them for others – sometimes using the symbolic language and images they are conveyed in, such as in some art, poetry, and channellings, and sometimes using more basic terms, for example when leading a workshop or working with a client. The use of more symbolic or surreal language and imagery in poems, songs, or art, allows readers, listeners, and observers some ambiguity so that they can interpret them according to their own needs, or means of understanding. When teaching it is more useful to be precise, however, it is important to remain aware that different people will need different slants to their lessons, so it is helpful to understand their needs fully. If working one-to-one, this is relatively easy, but if working with groups, you will need to incorporate specific elements to suit the needs of all your attendees.

The gates of altered states of consciousness are open for all who wish to enter in. If it is all new to you, it is good to start gradually in a safe environment, ideally with someone present who can help guide you to prevent any confusion. You need to know about grounding and protection as a minimum, and hopefully some basic techniques. I hope you will aim to achieve this sense of balance before frolicking too deep, to enable you to use your knowledge practically, to achieve aims, and even to shape the knowledge of humanity more accurately. You will then be a mutual co-creator of worlds, and the legends that go with them. Whatever you do I suggest that you always bear in your mind that you intend to be working with love and with lightness – keep your concentration and thoughts light, and try not to get too deeply sucked in too quickly. Also try not to judge what anyone needs. Sometimes things happen in very unexpected ways, but they make sense later if you trust your intuition to lead you.

When being objective, we can transcend and look back at our constructs with powerful clarity; instead of looking through them, which can give a murky and distorted view. We can then transform them into something new, to serve us better. We are not only liberated from old conventional illusions, but can go so far as to construct whatever other temporary illusions may be useful to us at that time in our journey – and re-mould them whenever and however we wish. Our minds are tools for seemingly pulling magic tricks on ourselves for our own good.

We can exist effectively in the supposed 'real' world, doing whatever job we choose and co-existing alongside whichever partner and within whatever social network we choose, as long as we believe it is the right thing for us to be doing at that time. If we feel that we have chosen how we live our lives, then we can remain happy with those choices, until such time as we decide to think differently and make any changes accordingly. If we have made our choices consciously, then we are also aware that it is usually better to find ways of dealing with any issues as harmoniously as possible, than to dive off sideways into some other choice that may well turn out to be a mistake, especially if it is a decision made as a hasty reaction. If you have chosen a certain job or partner very consciously then it is usually worth the effort to make those choices work. It's not as if issues disappear, but you learn to deal with them gently and intelligently, rather than carelessly and destructively. Remind yourself of the reasons for choosing them, and the other issues may fade into insignificance by comparison, but if there are still serious issues, then it is worth being courageous and honest in facing up to them fully. It is no good at all to let issues fester through not dealing with them, allowing resentments to build up. You may well even be surprised to find out how easily some things can be resolved if you open up and talk properly, especially if there have been assumptions and misunderstandings made.

    Good communication is always imperative in human relationships whether it be with a partner, friend, your child or another family member, your manager, or between countries. Good communication is something human beings are not that great at yet, and I think it still is one of our major stumbling blocks, but these are skills that can be learned. Hopefully if you have chosen your partner and friends well in the first place, so your communication levels should be reasonably on a par. Family members should also have some common level of understanding. Respect is a crucial factor; each party should be prepared to give the other time and space to speak and be listened to. If there is an issue with respect itself, then this is the first thing that needs to be sorted out, as it can destroy love, but love can conquer all if you get in there first. Clarity is always important so that you can get to the heart of the issue and not travel in emotionally exhausting circles. Take the time to try to prepare for an important discussion rather than try to do it off the cuff. Plan what the most important thing is for you to address, and do not be tempted to throw in all sorts of other snipes (which will only upset the applecart instead of getting it to its destination). Then choose a good time to have the discussion, even ask to book time for a chat (in a comfortable environment). It's not good trying to interrupt someone if they are busy with something else if you want their full attention. If you are struggling to even start an approach, you could use another level of consciousness first - to ask for help, to appeal to the other person's higher self, to be calm, grounded, confident, loving. You do this in a meditative state from a distance, without them even knowing, as if you are talking to them. Believe me this does work! You could even ask the other person to meditate with you to start with, to ask for help to communicate well (a bit like saying grace to bless your food and company). This means you are both committing to the aim. Let these magic realities filter back into your situation. Dream it well.

Waking from the dream of your life enough to look at it objectively allows you to analyse where changes may be desirable then, possibly with the help of extra tools, you can consciously begin to make those changes. To start with you may need to persevere determinedly – following plans (for example that a life coach may help you set up). It isn't all tough though, there are rewards along the way, and you need to be realistic – not ask yourself to do too much all at once, plus ask someone to be there for you if you need support along the way. Ask your friends and family to be understanding with you while you go through your changes too – for example if you are giving up smoking, do ask your visiting friends not to smoke in your living room during that time! Don't be too tough on yourself if you relapse a bit either, just get back on track as soon as you can. I have done such plans for myself on such topics as "getting fit & losing weight", "managing finances & paying off credit cards", "planning workshops from initial idea to completion", "following a study routine", etc – and there are many other areas of change this can work for.

When you feel like you are getting close to where you want to be, doing what you want to be doing with your life – then you can surrender the ego further – thus becoming more liberated and serene. Your life becomes more like a dream - relaxed, yet with you in control of its progression. Obviously you still need to make plans such as how to run a workshop, but they require less effort. You are more confident about the process. You can decide what you want to come into your dream, and by thinking it, you actively dream it to be so.

Previously we did think our dreams (and our lives), but we were not aware enough of our thoughts, so we threw in all sorts of confused rubbish. Perhaps then we needed to learn lessons from some of the things that we threw in our paths. We still do learn lessons, but everything now is so more consciously done – we can decide the whole thing – a lesson might even be a test to see if what we thought does in fact come out in a certain way – or to test our own progress. For example, when we say we are now a master of something, the universe seems to ask us to prove it, by giving us a situation in which we can show that it is true, or show that we really mean to follow a decision, no matter what tricks might be pulled out of the box!

Is it the universe, or is it ourselves dreaming the universe, and thus testing ourselves? Either way, we now know what it is like to actually experience being that 'master'! And the universe also knows what it is like for us to experience that.

I conclude that consciousness is at the root of everything. Consciousness pervades the 'realities' we dream, whether we are awake or asleep, or meditating, or whether we are experiencing a shamanic like journey to a seemingly separate world – we are merely in different levels of the same dream of everything. And maybe what we dream even expands the infinity of consciousness, if such dreams didn't exist before we thought of them.

Our dreams are personal to us – coloured by our upbringing, cultural background and language, beliefs, values, studies, past and current experiences, perception, etc – but there does also seem to be a collective dream containing collective historical and current knowledge (which we can tap into), and symbols which mean certain things to us.

Perhaps then there is also a cosmic dream that contains all of the aforementioned and more…. such as what Einstein tapped into when riding his light-beam, and many other scientists seem to tap into for new ideas. Often a new invention or breakthrough has come about at the same time in different parts of the world, as if communicated across the ether. In any case, as we evolve our state of being as humans (including practicing spiritual concepts perhaps, or studying, using the internet etc), so our capacity to evolve our states of consciousness increases. As we become more and more aware of what we are doing, the ability to *consciously* evolve our consciousness instead of randomly progressing also increases.

We don't really have any useful or meaningful ways to make the transition into adulthood in our society, and this often results in a lack of understanding, confusion, disconnection, and emotional anguish. There are details on how to help more with this in a guide available via my website. I believe we can bring elements of ancient wisdom, such as coming of age rituals as used in tribal customs, into a workshop setting in a powerful blend with modern personal development/growth concepts to provide a hugely supportive, creative and richly informed, meaningful and celebratory transition, which values and honours change, and increases understanding of it.

The workshops would ideally involve a team of people to provide a wide range of input, including therapeutic and indoor and outdoor creative sessions. Many topics should be covered, such as: Identity, Belonging, Responsibility, Communication, Relationships, Finance, Environment, Feelings, and Purpose or Aims in life. Meditation sessions, and some Shamanic Vision Questing work, to examine deeper levels of consciousness and self, should also be included. All of this grounds the physical and mental being, and gives the emotional being tools to cope with most eventualities.

The word 'Shaman' originates from the tribal language of Eastern Siberia, but the practice has been used in indigenous tribes all around the world – another very intriguing example of how similar things can happen in different places simultaneously without any of our normal forms of communication having taken place between the different groups! The practitioners use an altered state of consciousness to reach understanding and heal, in connection with the earth, plants, animals, and the elements of the natural world. Even in modern western poetry we might easily identify with a panther prowling in the night, or a bird flying over the mountains or sea, or a lion lazing in the sun, or a fish swimming up current in a stream beneath windswept willow trees. And in our collective psyches there are many meaningful symbols that can emerge to assist us with understanding abstract and conceptual ideas and feelings. They can also help us by bringing information from our subconscious to our conscious levels for attention.

While shamans often made use of substances normally derived from local plants to help them reach altered states of consciousness (as well as drumming and dancing), I do not believe that we have to do things this way at all if we know how to use our minds alone to get there. However, as we are examining altered states in this section, this is an area I could not justifiably ignore, and I think that there are some very interesting points to look at.

A brief look at the use of substances in relation to altered states of consciousness:

In "The World of Shamanism" Roger Walsh MD, PH.D. discusses whether psychedelics and entheogens can reveal the divine within –

produce similar mystical experiences to those experienced by spiritual practitioners of meditation for example. It seems there is no doubt that they can – however it will only happen sometimes to some people under certain circumstances.

The main problems are that drug use tends to produce inconsistent results, and can have harmful side effects on your physical, mental, and emotional health. Drug induced experiences also tend not to produce lasting awareness and learning in themselves, and may cause erratic behaviour, addiction, and chaos in the unwary, so may deteriorate your life rather than enhance it. However, it is of course possible to have an amazing epiphany, and instead of just forgetting it, respond to it by making positive changes in your life. I do know people who have had mystical experiences via drug use as well as via spiritual practice, so have a bit of an understanding of both sides of the coin. Also, some well known figures have used substances to help them achieve breakthroughs or to carry out studies (Newton, Casteneda, Huxley…..). I would thus argue that if someone is spiritually aware in the first place and then chooses to use drugs with a specific and positive intention in mind, they are likely to be more prepared to produce good results.

- They would tend to use the drugs in a more considered and deliberate way.
- They would tend to take precautions to prepare a safe environment, such as a quiet space with someone on standby to assist if necessary.
- They would tend to be more careful about using the correct amount and to ensure that the substance was pure.
- They would tend to avoid mixing substances such as alcohol and drugs.
- They would enter their altered state with focused intention.
- They may be able to use spiritual practice to ensure they achieve what they want to achieve – whether simply to experience a euphoric state, or whether to gain answers to questions, solve riddles, explore, come up with new ideas, etc.
- They may be attentive enough to record during or directly after the experience – what is happening or has happened, and thus learn more from it. (They could record things on a tape, or ask a friend to write down what they say.)

- They are more likely to monitor their use and not just indiscriminately take whatever is around at a party for example.
- They may be more likely to be mentally & emotionally balanced in the first place, so negative side effects would be less likely.
- They may be more aware of physical health too, keeping fit, eating healthily, drinking water, detoxifying, and resting when needed, plus taking breaks to guard against addictions – so the overall effect would be less destructive.

As Louis Pasteur said, "Chance favours a prepared mind", so if we are aware of what we are doing and why etc, we can achieve much better results than if we just use drugs to experience temporary states in a random way.

Nihilism, and the need to know the SELF so that you can be true to it.

This is something that tends to come up with anyone exploring consciousness and the meaning of life, particularly with intelligent and sensitive people. Coming up against a world full of apparently 'good' and 'bad' things (and other paradoxes), and trying to decide how to choose & act in the face of the mystery of life, can present quite a painful dilemma. If we are not sure what life means, then how do we know what to choose? What does it really matter? Wouldn't it just be better to get drunk and try and forget it? Or keep too busy to think? No, of course not – as these questions will always return in the end – so it's better to just try to get on with it. Surely they cannot be too fearsome to face? Of course it's okay to do it gradually, give yourself time to come to terms with things.

If it is up to us to choose what is important / how we should exist – then we need to reach some clarity about what life means to us *personally*.

Many of us are brought up within some sort of belief system or at least with some sort of philosophy concerning what life is about. Often we accept these, and other times we wish to change them, as our experiences lead us to believe differently. Sometimes we just don't think about it until later, perhaps something happens to make us stop, and try to take stock of where we are at. If our upbringing and/or schooling has not been kind to us, we may find ourselves drifting, not sure what we want to do with our lives, or if we have come out of a sad or painful marriage for example, or are bereaved, and are trying to start again, then we may need some help to find our way. There are plenty of professionals able to help you get some perspective on things, and it is a sensible and logical thing to ask for help rather than struggle on alone. Try to find a professional who seems as if they might resonate with the kind of person you are, and if one doesn't work out, do move on to a different one, it's important to get it right for your own sake.

If we believe we have done everything right, and then become disillusioned, not wanting to continue along that path, then this too can present huge problems. But if you know you want to change, why not just seek help to change, instead of making it a painful thing. Perhaps you expected yourself to be perfect? No one is perfect in that sense, we all need to adjust as we grow and learn, but we are all perfect as human beings, here to do precisely that, grow and learn, and choose how we wish to experience life

Some choices are more obvious than others – we know we need a job to pay for somewhere to live, and our regular bills, for example – this is about basic survival. We know we need to speak with our partner to resolve a problem (though we may still seek help in how best to do that if it is tricky). We can see that our child has an issue at school and can help get that resolved, etc; but there are also less obvious things we need to make choices about. It's very important to be conscious of our everyday health for example. Good diet and exercise makes a big difference, so does not putting too much rubbish into our systems. Good physical, mental, and emotional health, helps us to look at life positively, and aim to get something out of it, whether that be to study for a certain career, travel and explore, or to have children, or to help a charity, for example, these are all meaningful things. If we suspect that we might be feeling lethargic or depressed due to a lack of something in our diet, or if we suspect an allergy, then we can use kinesiology (muscle testing which shows your body's response to things) for example, to tell us where a weakness reflects an intolerance or lack, and then make changes accordingly. We can use a life coach or counsellor to help us discover what it is we really want to do with our lives, and then plan to make changes needed to achieve that. We can use a counsellor of course to help us resolve any emotional issues getting in our way. We can use a diviner to help us find out many hidden things about ourselves and our environment.

We can use a healer to bring healing, along with feedback as to why things may be the way they are and what we can do to help ourselves recover better. We can use yoga or tai chi etc, not only to keep supple, but also to sense what is going on in our bodies, where tensions lie, and even why. Getting enough sleep is obviously important too, but be careful not to go too far the other way as many people make this mistake. If you sleep too much it can make you feel very lethargic.

At the end of the day we are all individuals with the right to make choices that are personal to us, but at the same time we are part of the human race, as well as part of the life on this planet, so we have a responsibility to try not to harm others or our environment.

Finding a way to make your own choices that are also okay generally, gives one a sense of personal power and validation in life. Trying to live with too much compromise on our morals, beliefs, and sense of self can be very uncomfortable indeed.

Some other things that may hold us back from living consciously satisfying lives.

If you feel guilty about something you have done then you need to find a way to move past that. Confessing to it is a possible way to release tension, or think what you might have done to cause the situation, then figure out if there is a way you can put it right. This might include damage to ourselves that we are unaware of, for example the body may become sick to force us to stop working if we badly need a rest, or a chance to think about making changes in our lives.

Sometimes things in the past are not redeemable, so we need to learn to accept this and let it go. Hopefully you might have learnt something from it. Some things may not have truly been your 'fault', especially if you did try your best at the time – so let go of these too, and forgive yourself for holding onto that pain in the first place. It's easier to see mistakes in hindsight, but you should forgive yourself for not knowing better in the past.

If you are feeling bad about something that you should not really be blamed for, then you may be allowing someone else to have power over you – so it's a question of facing up to how to claim back one's own power. People can so easily lay blame on us, consciously or unconsciously, if we let them, so don't allow this.

Remember that you do need to take care of yourself. You cannot expect to help anyone else or do anything useful if you don't take care of yourself. This just means in a functional sort of way, it does not mean being selfish. So while you may have done something to upset someone else for example, it rather depends if you have deliberately done it out of selfishness, spite etc, or if there really was no choice because you could not accept the situation. Or perhaps it was an oversight or a misunderstanding and you did not realise you were hurting someone until afterwards.

Behaviour is an issue that can be corrected – it is separate from the person – the person is love, loves, and is loved, regardless – we are all perfect in the sense that we are human beings making human mistakes, and hopefully learning from them. Behaviour can be put into perspective and adjusted, but each party needs to retain their own sense of being themselves – true to themselves – one should not be subjugated to another's wishes – they should only seek to compromise where possible (both ways) for the best of both parties. Sometimes one has to explain why one cannot submit to another's needs. We are not there to fit other people's needs; only to be ourselves to the best of our ability. If we can see where a compromise might work, then well and good, but if one person is expecting unreasonable demands from the other, then we should stand up for ourselves. **We need to respect our true selves, and then others will also be more likely to respect us too.** If we give in then we will tend to lose that respect and almost invite further erosion of the situation. Respect for each other is paramount. If you work from this basis then it should become obvious how to achieve balance. Each party should want the other to be their true self, and thus give them the trust and freedom to be so. Being respectful means listening to each other's points of view and trying to understand. Issues that come up in any form of relationship are almost never entirely arising from the behaviour of only one party. Usually as they say, "it takes two to tango". Both parties just need to try to understand what has happened, and why, then they can work out (hopefully without blame) how to rectify things and re-affirm their love, or if it comes to that, decide not to continue.

In any case guilt is negative, and like worry, does not serve any useful purpose other than to point out to you that there is something that needs attention. Once it is given attention with the aim to resolve it then it should no longer be allowed to eat away at you, and should be set aside, as the job of making you aware has been done. You should move on to find resolutions, not waste any further time or energy on it.

If someone succeeds in making us feel guilty, it may be from their own fear that you cannot be who they want you to be. If someone is looking for you to fulfil a need in them, or fill an empty space in them, then this needs to be sorted out. Two people can only continue to be in a close long term relationship if they are able to get on with each other as their true selves. There should be no manipulation to try to get someone else to be what you think you need. Each party needs to be accepted for who they really are – it is no good trying to squeeze them into your mould. On the other hand of course, it does not mean they can totally disregard your feelings and walk all over you! If you are to share space then both parties need due consideration, so you do need to compromise to some degree, but only to a reasonable and practical level. (This can be more difficult if one party moves in with the other, as they have pre-established rules or habits regarding their territory that it is difficult for the incoming party to ask them to change, yet some compromise is necessary or the incoming party will feel disrespected, and possibly even as though they don't truly belong there. Obviously the thing is not to be unreasonable and expect too much. Just focus on what is most important to you.)

Fear is one of the biggest things that gets in our way, but there is no need to fear. We are all just trying to learn how to be who we are and can be. No one should be judging you or anybody, and if they are, then that is their problem, not yours. Just don't let their opinions bother you – it is your opinion of yourself that matters. Sometimes we even judge ourselves too harshly, as long as we are trying things, and learning as we go, then all is well. People who really love you, such as partners, family, friends, only want to help, so try not to be defensive about anything they might point out – try to just give what they say fair consideration and then decide for yourself if you need to take any of it on board or not. Don't feel you have to keep trying to please everybody, or to prove yourself to others – just aim to be comfortable yourself with who you are.

Naming Ceremonies are used in some countries, often among the more indigenous peoples, which are a beautiful way to handle things. When a child is born, a special deeply meaningful name is chosen not just by the parents, but by the wider circle of family and friends, and sung to them. If someone transgresses as they grow up, then the community sings their name to them again to remind them who they really are. It is also sung to you at celebrations to mark important events in your life, to celebrate your essential self and

encourage you to be the best you can be. **Our best friends always reflect back to us who we truly are.** Even in western culture, if you say something out of place in public, then imagine the look your best friend would probably give you, to say "Gee that doesn't sound like you my friend, what is going on?" Trust your friends to help you keep on track, don't be angry with them for trying to help you. Don't fear they will judge you. They are only questioning the behaviour of the moment. Wouldn't you want to be able to do the same thing for them?
Be who you feel deeply you are meant to be, it is the only truly real way to live, and indeed also the only true way to love.

Tell the voice of fear within you to stop wasting your time, when you could be getting on and doing something new.

Seek help with self empowerment, wisdom to help you choose, tools to help you adjust to change, and to support you.

Sacred Perspectives

Abraham Maslow (often quoted in Social Services Training due to his pyramid diagram showing the hierarchy of need, with the basic needs such as food and shelter occupying the base level, a lot in-between, and spiritual need for self-actualisation at the top), said "without the transcendental and the transpersonal, we get sick, violent, nihilistic, or else hopeless and apathetic". We need the spiritual to be fully balanced as people. There are many areas you can explore without commitment.

Spiritual therapy relieves the sense of alienation and estrangement from the universe and everything around us. It creates a sense of connection and alignment with the sacred, fostering a transpersonal and trans-egoic sense of identity, and it also helps repair & harmonize relationships, and stabilize social structures or networks.

It also brings deeply meaningful experiences of the creative, and of life, into society. (The amount or type of neurotransmitter enzymes can apparently be thrown out of balance by stress – and be brought back into balance by meditation for example.) **Meditation is a most wonderful tool for helping us to help ourselves.**

Dis-ease can be greatly reduced via healing of the **subjective emotional states**, plus mental, and physical situations, and permanent changes in the health of mind/body/spirit can be brought into effect.

Active Spirituality

Invite the Sacred to melt your stress, inspiring you to rise above the subjective, and empowering you to focus clearly on achieving what you intend. Re-connect with the universe, your creativity and sense of divine expression, and enjoy the world and people around you more. Use your awareness to take note of the amazing details, sensations, and beauty all around you. Find more peace, love, & balance at the physical, mental, and emotional levels. Discuss choices, share tools, journey with confidence to discover your innate uniqueness alongside a sense of deep belonging.

Use of Intuition and Consciousness leads to a Trust in Self

Mentastics (Mental Gymnastics) is a system where you use your intuition to sense what is working well for your body and to move in ways which are good for it (stretching things that need stretching, adjusting to regain good posture, or even moving differently to cope with a handicap). Open your mind, set aside ego, let the universe in to inspire you. Breathe deeply. Use your mind as a tool. Ask yourself "What can be lighter, more free feeling?" and you will find yourself moving more lightly and freely. Some athletes use this to get into 'the Zone'. You can use meditation to entrain your mind to slow and relax so that you can listen more to the intuitive voice within you. Place one hand on your heart and one on your throat to help calm and heal, and awaken your own potential. As you learn to trust your intuition so it will help you more and more.

- In your true self you can communicate with lack of fear, for you are being who you really are and asking to be respected and listened to as that person. You cannot be responsible for the listener's chosen behaviour, but you can hope for the best either way. They are more likely to respect you and listen, but if they do not, then you can forgive them for being so unconscious and let them go in peace, as you know you have tried your best. If they understand, then you have something to move forward with together.
- Responsibility can joyously be taken for choices made and choices to be decided upon.
- You can learn to help yourself heal – emotionally & physically.

- You can learn to use your mind as a tool for your own benefit instead of letting it rule.
- You can rise above the subjective and see the bigger picture.
- Illness might be healed, guilt assuaged, relationships harmonized, and even death's sting soothed.
- You can accept what needs to be accepted and find ways of coping.
- You can surrender your ego to become part of the huge buzzing energy of the universe & find answers to many questions, yet at the same time be calm & become even more of your true unique self.
- You feel lucid and at home. You discover where you are & where you are going, and become full of ideas to help you on your way.

A state of ECSTASY can be gained through Laughter or Movement (dancing, long distance running or swimming, etc), or singing, or playing an instrument, or in fact doing anything you really love doing; as well as through stillness – being in a meditative or contemplative state. Although you can be walking for example, your mind can still be linked to the stillness within yourself and the universe. Also contemplating positives such as your skills, your partner's good points, being grateful, being part of the universal stream of life, nature, art, etc, helps to maintain a sense of ongoing grace.

Confront any shadows in your psyche until dissolved / accepted – then you will fear them no more either in yourself or others. **Don't disown or repress dark thoughts, work to understand then release them.** You can also use your shadow side to express yourself through writing or art for example. Even if you feel very empty or bleak, this can helps to work things through. At the very least you are doing something active to process the stage instead of letting it swamp you, and probably helping it to pass quicker. It can be like going through a tunnel until you find there is daylight again on the other side.

Journey on behalf of humanity. Light up what others see as darkness. Self-centred striving ceases if you can find the centre of calm strength within yourself. Use whatever self-help tools you can find that work for you. Write down positive things to remind you what you want to do, and be, and what your strengths and skills are. Be self fulfilled. Helping yourself helps others, and helping others helps yourself (if you are first of all strong enough to not let it drain you). Be in a state of Grace. Grace is a word we can keep in our minds to enhance our intentions – when we walk, dance, swim, talk, sing, do anything at all – to enable us to get in 'the zone' where everything flows more easily – where everything feels lighter, and we are in a peak state. Grace allows us to follow our inner guidance – be true to who we are – and give our gifts lightly to the world. It's one of those magic words you can sing to yourself! We can all be instruments of Grace – adding to human consciousness.

Deep Consciousness means Open Heartedness. This allows the higher spiritual energy centres of your upper body to flow through freely to harmonize with the lower physical centres. **Spiritual Relationships encourage you to bring more meaning into life.**

Work with love, remember why you are here, what your unique talent is. Ask yourself what you are here to do, what your true purpose is. This is not necessarily a particular vocation, but might be a 'soul developmental lesson' for example. People always know what they want but often do not allow themselves to trust that they do know, or are afraid to commit to it.

Gandhi said "My life is my message" – the same is true for all of us. To know it and live it, gives us power, helps us choose who we want to show up as.

We hold silence and songs bursting to become real. When we respond with open hearts we say YES to ourselves, and this is reflected in our whole demeanour and attitude, so others find us attractive. When we live aware lives, enjoying our experience of life, that is also apparent to others as an inherent sensuality. When we approach life with a defensive heart, we seek love yet cannot receive it.

Try this chant, using whatever tones or notes you like – *"Mey hey – my world is beautiful. Mey hey – today is beautiful. Wah hey – everything is beautiful – today."* Then we can sing it again tomorrow, and feel it to be more true each day. You are making it true in fact.

Successful communication is imperative in relationships. Assume the other has good intentions and are doing the best they can. Speak to others as you would have them speak to you, respectfully. Begin by expressing appreciation so they will feel received and heard – don't learn this the hard way because then it's too late. Be clear about your purpose – be specific – express the facts. Don't muddy the situation with irrelevant details. Share your truth from your heart – without blame. Half a dozen sentences are enough at a time – then be silent and let it sink in. Then listen. Give them a space. Breathe deeply and slowly. Welcome the person and the moment into your heart. Remember that all are teachers. Stay open and be present.

I do have some meditations for couples in a guide, especially ones suitable for affirming that you are willing to work together on a deeper level. You can make up very simple ceremonies yourself, touch each other's hearts and promise to be there for each other to the best of your ability, for example.

Guilt and worry are totally useless emotions, thus a waste of energy to indulge in. Yes we can notice that we have a concern but then we do something about it, we move forwards positively – even if it is just to make a list – that at least lets us clear our heads from it swimming around distracting us, and gives us steps to take. Yes we can notice that we might feel guilty about something, but again, we can take steps to change that instead of focusing on the feeling.

If someone else is trying to make us feel guilty, then we must remember that it is only the behaviour and not the person (in both parties), and again take steps to either speak about it to resolve the issue, or take steps to change what you think needs changing. Don't let someone else pile guilt onto you unjustly; you can gently say to them that you do not feel as if you should own that guilt and why you think it is not fair; then you can think about steps together to change that situation to the benefit of both of you.

Don't allow others to manipulate you through unjustly loading you up with emotions. Don't be afraid to calmly point out that this is not useful to either of you.

Treat guilt or worry simply as feelings that make us aware of something that needs discussing or acting upon, and move on from the feeling itself, to the action.

Forgiveness is something we can learn to do, until eventually the need for it might not even arise. If you are able to love unconditionally, you will not judge or hold painful grudges. You accept that things are as they are without trying to apportion blame, and therefore will have no need for forgiveness as such. You may still feel sad that things are that way, but if there is nothing you can do about it, then you accept that you have to leave it be. One who truly loves has already forgiven others and themselves along the way. This is of course an ideal we can work towards.

Only in our hearts can we embrace and resolve the paradoxes that bewilder our minds. In every moment we have a choice – to contract our hearts in fear or expand them with love. When we make the choice to forgive, we transcend the temptation to cling to anger which only hurts us if we do. If you hold onto pain then you are actually giving the other person power over you. Surrender it so that you can heal.

Forgiveness is a simple step we will take when we are ready to leave behind pain, rage, sorrow, bitterness – and unburden our hearts to become light and peaceful. After all what good can it possibly do us to cling to these hurtful emotions? Take responsibility for your part in these dramas and apologise to the other as well as to yourself. This does not mean that you sanction the actions that caused the pain in the first place, but just that you wish to let them go and move beyond them, releasing it all, and thus releasing yourself from the angst.

Never hold onto resentments as they get more poisonous the longer you do. Talk them through to find solutions between you, or forgive and let go. (If you don't, you will build up painful blockages in the energy centre of the heart.) This doesn't mean you just forget, it means that you honour past differences and move on without holding resentment, but hopefully all parties learn from the experience, especially if you have managed to communicate clearly about what was going on as well. Sometimes people simply split up because they did not have the knowledge at the time to enable them to work things out. How can anyone be to blame for that? We are all learning as we go.

A compassionate transitional ritual to let go of a past relationship in a transforming way, is a great idea if at all possible – to acknowledge having been so much part of each other's lives and honour the original friendship there. Acknowledgement of what was good and precious from the past and seeing how this still helps today, rather than carrying wounds forward into next relationships, is a very healthy way to handle things. Thank each other for the experiences you brought into each other's lives, and release each other with blessings. Acknowledge your and the other's fear of being hurt & of showing emotion. If you cannot do any of this with the other person, then you can do it in a meditation where you simply allow your soul to speak to theirs. It may seem to be all in your imagination, but it makes a difference!

I still love the man, who gave me kids – why would I not, though we lost our bliss? We were hurting each other more than helping, so sadly, each had to be freed, to be the person they chose to be. He seemed to need to assume a role where he 'had to' suffer for the sake of love, which made me feel awful, as I so wanted him to be happy, but whatever I did was resented or mocked, and he wouldn't seek any outside help. After many years of very little communication, I felt so pushed away that I had to plan an exit. I knew we still loved each other, and it was all due to crazy misunderstandings, but as we couldn't sort it out, it was unbearable for us both.

If things don't work out, you can still love the person, even maybe be friends if you're lucky, as many manage to do. Ideally that's the healthy way to do things, but it doesn't happen if people hold onto pain, so then you have to try to let go of the whole situation, difficult though that is when there are always things to remind you of that sad waste.

    Sometimes it's hard to believe how unconscious we can be, especially in relationships. Living with someone all the time is just not easy, so it's no good just walking away and thinking it will be better with someone else. It is really worth trying to make what you have work out first, so that you don't have a chain of regrets to deal with as well as trying to start over again.

    Both parties need to work at things, and it's imperative to communicate with great consideration. I think good communication is something that human beings really struggle with, so it's worth seeking out wise help and advice (sooner rather than later, when too much has already been misunderstood, and resentments have built up), and really taking time to get this as right as you can, to give things the best chance they can have. A good counsellor can mediate if things have gotten a bit out of hand, to assist each to have their say and not rant on for ages. Or you can study communication advice and write notes or lists to plan priorities & approaches. Also, you have to stop being defensive to be able to deal with the challenges that might come up.

In conscious relationships, the **deep level of open hearted communication** between you and your partner should allow you to speak openly about past (and present) fears, hurts, or bad experiences. The actuality of creating such a deep heart-to-heart connection might provoke fears, as you may initially feel vulnerable or insecure. We should open to trust and let love heal. We really do have nothing to lose and everything to gain from being prepared to try again – fully. Speaking the truth is healing in itself. If we can feel more and more accepted, and thus become more spontaneous and relaxed rather than defensive, the 'demons' will slip away and be gone.

Surrender is essential to open the heart. People often think that surrender means loss of free will or personal power – but it does not mean this at all – it means to melt into that which is higher – to honour and welcome your highest potential and grow into it – so it actually gives you *more* free will and personal power. It gets our little ego based worries out of the way – because we realise that they are lower level and therefore not quite so relevant – we take note of them, but do not allow them to control us. It makes room for something much better.

Our love is a great leap of the heart – and we embrace what IS. It is a leap of faith despite our fears, into the innocence of new beginnings. By risking our hearts and opening to love, we taste essential freedom and joy. We develop the capacity to surrender to the flow of excitement without inhibition.

Breathe, feel the grace of love in your bellies, the centre of balance, rotate and sway the pelvis, tighten & relax muscles to keep supple, dance in ways that make every bit of you feel good. Be natural, loose and playful. Making sounds of delight gives flavour and colour to our energy and a message of approval to our partners. Let your wild self come out and even growl… be proud and strong about who you are and what you feel.

Joy is a spiritual practice, a form of prayer, we bring into our lives by affirming our love of life, our inherent perfection as created beings, who can also create in turn, and our completeness and freedom to be who we are.

Being in the present moment is a more joyful practice than hankering after the past or yearning for the future, or living with hopes and fears. If we can be grateful for what we have in the present then we are more joyful.

If we can embrace who we are at all levels of our being then we can be joyful and authentic. If we can relax into the flow of life, and be loving & trusting, then we can be joyful and powerful and balanced.

It takes courage to speak our truth, it is taking a risk to be authentic, but this is imperative in a good relationship. It is essential to be able to tell each other what you like & dislike, what you feel & think, without fear. It is essential to be able to express the mystery of life and love. When you tell each other how beautiful you are and what you love about each other, it gives you confidence. Love & cherish.

Create Special Moments. Special outings, playful times, writing, singing – all give special opportunities for joyful and creative communication with family members – lovers or children. Special moments created do not need to cost a lot. Be angels for each other always, precious angels.

It is important to check for feedback as you go along and don't just assume things are okay. You need to be able to speak freely about what didn't work as well as to express appreciation of what did work, so that you can learn and grow from the experience as a whole, and move into a place (as a couple) with even more potential for ecstasy. Keep it in balance and be gentle. Never judge or criticize one another, which can cause personal hurt - just talk in terms of the experience – trying to express feelings positively – and always be open to games or surprises. Let the experience infuse your everyday life, your meals, your conversations, the way you walk, dress, touch – say YES to a pleasurable life.

[Of course, good communication with your children and young people is very important too, and the more open you can be the better. I think that people often do not have enough full family discussions, but it seems fair to me that even the younger members of the family should be shown how things work in running a family and brought into at least some decision making processes. Surely it is all part of growing up, and if they don't learn about these things gradually then they might have a shock when they have to suddenly learn it all at once later on. They can usually understand more than we give them credit for, and it helps them to feel part of the team, and feel confident in being able to talk with you if there is something worrying them. Children, and particularly teenagers, should have the opportunity to be able to discuss their feelings, make input, and ask for understanding or explanations.]

If you have to have a difficult conversation, try to be objective rather than letting your subjective emotions distract you. Try to explain how you feel in a non-emotive, non-manipulative way, just being clear and honest. Ask for space to be listened to properly first if your partner tries to butt in, then give them space to express their point of view and try to understand that. We all see things very differently and it is best to try to see the bigger picture that includes other people's viewpoints and why misunderstandings might have happened. Try to remember that behaviour is a separate thing from the actual person, and so you can perhaps still show your love with a gentle touch while talking.

The deep trust and love that develops between you in a spiritual relationship also makes you so sure about your partnership that jealousy or insecurity are simply not issues that arise. You do not try to control each other, you trust each other to be the best you can be as partners in every sense of the word (lover, friend, partner in life). You also know that this means allowing them, and encouraging them, to pursue their own goals and life paths.

So you can enjoy particularly close friendships with others because you know your partner is not going to misread things and start acting all silly. And you will be freely trusted to follow your own needs in life – such as going out to run your workshops, or going out to play your music, without your partner wondering about what you might be up to! But although you are free to do what you need in life, remember you are also free to ask for support anytime, and also to ask for special time to enjoy together.

You will have simply reached levels of maturity where lower emotional mix-ups are forgotten things of the past. Loving each other fully and openly, and communicating well, are now the most important things in your relationship, so petty issues are easily dissolved by this powerful blending and bonding.

Be the love you wish to see in the world. Communicate, love, share, blossom! Live ON PURPOSE. Be like glowing candles.

Gratefulness Exercise:

Write down things you are grateful for (a whole family can do this together). This is a great way to remind yourselves of the positives in your lives, and can open up some interesting discussions. It is surprisingly easy to realize how minor negatives can be if you focus on the positives. Telling your kids, or your partner, what you appreciate really makes them feel valued. If all we do is moan about the mess or the chores not done, then we should not be surprised if they don't want to be around us much.

Points to ponder when trying to achieve something:

- Don't blame others for negativity – be a quiet example.

- Forgive them for they (sometimes) know not what they do.
- Don't judge & don't let judgments others might make affect you.
- Keep focused on what you want to achieve by going step by step – keeping positive momentum.
- Ask for support from wherever you need it.
- Clarity is paramount, so list what you want to achieve (also possibly things like Why, How, When). The same applies if you want to ask someone else to do something.

Positivity Exercise:

Look at these examples and then make up some affirmations personal to yourself. They must be in the **present tense.** You can access many more generalised **affirmations** via my website. There are also plenty of **visualizations** there. There are more of both later in this book too.

- I am a helpful person / teacher / parent / partner / teenager
- I am a considerate & understanding parent / teenager / friend / partner
- I take responsibility for myself and make my own choices.
- I keep taking steps to learn more, and share inspiring information.
- Helping others heightens my vibrations.
- New ideas heighten my vibrations.
- I respond intuitively to do or say the most appropriate things.
- I appreciate the beautiful world around me, my family and friends, and am grateful for my skills, and the opportunity to use and extend them.

Observe things in daily life in more detail, and practice visualisations

Visualisations are like movies you create in your mind to help you feel good. We use what we have experienced to make these up, so the more optimally we learn how to use all our senses to observe things fully in normal states of consciousness, the better. Practice looking at things in great detail – a stone, a leaf, an insect for example – record all things you notice, using all the senses, tiny details and any creative additions. What are your thoughts in relation to things you discover?

The more you hone your senses, the better your visualizations will become. It's like exercise for the imagination. The better we visualize, the better we can be aware of what we are doing too. Imagine new worlds in the morning, new songs to dance out, new dreams to fly with, new joys to delight in.

Visualisations can be used for many purposes. If we visualise well, our minds treat it like a real experience and respond accordingly, so we can relax by imagining ourselves in a beautiful natural spot, satisfy our curiosity by exploring a situation or an imagined area, or revitalise ourselves through a vigorous imagined experience.

We can also use visualisation to anticipate how we may feel in a given situation and thus work out how best to deal with it and literally practice being in that situation, or we can even work out how to get into a desired position. A desired position could be anything from finding more work or getting a promotion to going on a hike or a holiday, to developing an attribute or skill. We can also reach a better understanding of how others might feel in any given situation through visualisation.

Life by Design

Further exploration of the differences and similarities between various altered states of consciousness.

This part is written in response to what I was reading in The World of Shamanism book I mentioned earlier (by Roger Walsh), where comparisons were being made between different states of consciousness to show that what a Shaman does is different from for example a Yogi or a Buddhist. My own experiences tend to show up aspects of all of these, and other states, so I agree that there are various different altered states, but at the same time I see no reason why one person cannot access all those differing states for different purposes. Forgive me for writing of my own experiences, but that is what I know, although of course I accept that you may have very different experiences.

My altered states of consciousness seem to be more like those described as shamanism (when journeying) than those of a yogi a lot of the time, but it depends a lot on what my aim is, and I do experience other states at other times. I previously thought that they were all more similar, but now I am happy to accept that there is some distinction between them, although I think that they may tend to blend somewhat, with very little sense of boundary between them.

I am generally able to maintain a high degree of control and can organize my progress and communicate with others present, or write things down, while at the same time being 'elsewhere' (although initial attempts may have been slightly erratic). I can concentrate at the same time on what I am doing, but it is not a heavy concentration, it is a light one! I find this is often an area of misunderstanding – most people seem to think that the concentration needed for extra-sensory work, or indeed for any meditation even, is hard and difficult to achieve. I find that trying too hard to concentrate can actually stop the whole altered state shift from happening. The concentration level needed is a soft, light, gentle, flowing one. If you smile to yourself while attempting this it might help achieve the right state, even move your head a bit as if you are out on a lovely walk! Think of the word GRACE, I find that is a fantastic word for getting the right feel. A healer is an instrument of grace and brings that sense of grace to their client. This even works when studying.

I don't feel depleted or fatigued after any altered state of consciousness episode. The energy flows through me constantly from the source, so that I am in fact replenished, rather than using up my own reserves.

Occasionally I work in situations (such as soul rescue or crime investigations) which can seem scary, but I know that fear can cause panic. I remind myself that non-judgement & unconditional love dissolve fear, so as long as I stay with a loving perspective, I know I am safe. I also know that deep down everything stems from the same original stream of consciousness, although some bits can get very lost, and I should not allow myself to be caught out by forgetting this.

In states such as journeying, or emptying the mind, your altered state can be even deeper as one is more free to let go. Some states are active, and others are very still. In dowsing we walk around to find things, although you can start by standing in one spot to take direction and distance readings where appropriate. When we have found the exact spot we wanted we then stand still to take detailed measurements.

I can be excited and hugely energized at the same time as immensely calm and grounded. What I show to clients is the calm and grounded side. My emotions and focus flow with the flow of the journey. Even when doing advanced meditation, things flow from having thoughts to having no thoughts, and then when my personal mind is emptied, the whole universe seems to have room to come in, so it is a surrender or a letting go in order to allow space for more (a bit like clearing out cupboards).

When I first started this type of meditation, I used to imagine putting my thoughts gently aside on a shelf, and then I began imagining I was wrapped in a cloud, or stepping out of a gate (in a high wall) into mist, to help reduce sense-stimulation, so these are helpful techniques. The gate gives your mind a clear prompt to move from one state to another. You may like to imagine walking though a wood to relax you before arriving at the gate in the wall. When the mind lets go of all its clutter enough, it becomes one with the flux of the whole universe, and is also open to any insight or experience that might prove relevant or useful at that time.

When I am journeying, I do feel as if I am travelling over great distances at great speeds, like a Shaman, and can do amazing things. I feel light and light-hearted, like a laugh or a dance. However, I do not seem to be actually *separated* from my body as there is no sense of having left it behind as such, but I often seem to become blended with something else, or a whole series of other things, with no limits really. I have had a couple of times where someone else was leading a group meditation where I separated at least partially from my body, so I know what that feels like, and I never get that feeling when doing my own journeying. Perhaps this is because I don't really feel separated, even in 'real' life, from the world around me (particularly the natural world). I do still have my identity, but this feeling of being part of everything, and thus ultimately safe, has always been part of that identity.

Shamanism has been practiced by many 'primitive' cultures around the world, and their differing cultures do seem to have influenced their experiences of journeying, yet they are fundamentally shamanistic in nature.

I seem to differ from this in that I don't have very much idea about a specific cosmology – I do not have any sort of cultural map of places and things to guide me. My experiences do not arise from any set of beliefs. My understanding of the symbology of any experience does not arise from any set system, however I do think there is a whole lot of symbology available to us in the collective consciousness which crosses the boundaries of cultures, times, locations, identities etc. I believe I access this as a poet, especially if writing surreal poetry, and where I use language differently. The experience always seems multi-sensory, colourful, and coherent, whether complex or simple.

Ramtha says that *the true you is unseen, like the wind or a thought, we have bodies so that we can express ourselves on this plane. He says that our purpose is to make known the unknown.*

 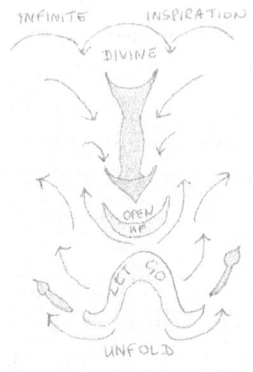 

Multidimensional Senses

In "The Fragrant Mind (Aromatherapy for Personality, Mind, Mood, and Emotion)", Valerie Ann Worwood says that "we do not understand much about how aroma molecules translate into smell, but that olfaction research involves chemistry, stereochemistry (the shape of molecules), vibrational frequency, electro-chemical factors, enzymes and proteins, and a whole lot more besides – therefore it is multidimensional in a way that sight and hearing are not".

However, I would consider all our senses to be multidimensional. There seem to be different layers of taste, for example at outset, then as you proceed to eat, then afterwards – like with wine – and we can often pick up traces of each component of a dish. Things taste different according to what they are mixed with, for example fruit in a curry as opposed to on its own or with cereal or yoghurt. For some people at least, taste is a trigger for memories in a similar way to smell, especially of childhood memories, of things you might never otherwise remember. Like any sense, taste can be trained / developed, and its language understood.

We can use both to good effect in visualisations, instead of just relying on sight, hearing, and touch.

Taste and smell must be interlinked in a huge way every day of our lives. Even if something tastes fine it is almost impossible to drink it if it smells weird. Touch and sight come into our appreciation of food and so much more. Textures can put you off eating something just as easily as bad presentation or discolouration, or they can feel good. A good crunchy raw carrot might even appeal to you on a sound level as well as texture and colour wise.

As a healer I find that touch, sight, and hearing are immensely multidimensional. I get all sorts of things happening at different levels.

I think we must somehow tune into different frequencies, a bit like picking up extra wavelengths on a radio, particularly when tuned in to a client or a situation. Another way of putting it might be that it's kind of like being in a zone (like an athlete or a fast driver) might be, where we perform at optimum levels.

People often recognise that they might have experienced extra sensory sensations if they have been driving fast for example. You might suddenly get a feeling that you need to slow down – and sure enough there turns out to be an accident or something ahead. Often it's a feeling I don't know how to describe, just a "knowing", that we tend to listen to. Sometimes it is like a gentle touch, sometimes more like a shout, and sometimes a picture comes into your head. I think this is because when we are driving fast we are (hopefully) in the light state of concentration where we can achieve optimum focus.

When divining for water we can literally see and feel under the ground, and get a sense of textures, and even tastes of what the rock and the water are like. At other times, such as when divining on an archaeological site, I might get a whole film going on in my head, where it is just as if I am standing there watching a village that was there ages ago, going through a day, with all the sounds, movements, smells, temperatures, etc in huge detail.

Sometimes if someone says to me – oh, I've lost my ring, I think I must have dropped it in town for example, then I might get a picture of a piece of furniture flash into my head, so I can say "No, I think it's at home" and I can describe its whereabouts to her, and sure enough it will be there. I was a bit puzzled by a piano stool once – describing it as a sort of thing at chair level opening like a cupboard but upwards! She knew at once what I meant. I've done these sort of things over the phone too, identifying a bag like a swimming cap, or a basket, where things were to be found, or that something had fallen down behind a pot plant or chair, or been left somewhere else.

I don't walk around picking up such details. That would be totally overwhelming, so I kind of screen out things, but my senses are immediately triggered into action by a sort of question, or it can come into play if something seems important…. Like with the driving thing. Obviously if I am tuning in for healing, divining, or seeking information then I am switching it on. Someone once walked across the room to me at a party and asked if I knew what was wrong with him, and my answer was "Well I do now that you have asked the question" and he blushed as it was an embarrassing thing.

These sensitivities of sight and touch, hearing etc, extend to anything really – I might pick up information about a plant I walk past – it might seem to call out for attention, so I might return to it and perceive that it needs something, or could be used for something, or just that it is particularly beautiful. Animals might show me that they need healing, and where, either by 'getting inside my head' or by coming up to me and presenting me with the afflicted area. This has included wild animals as well as domestic, particularly as a child, before I had even trained as a healer.

We can read things in people's faces or bodies to a huge extent anyway if we look. The expression "It was written all over them" really does mean it was obvious, but it's a combination of our senses that pick up on that information…. The drooped shoulders, the dishevelled clothes, the listless speech, that certain scent a depressed person seems to exude from their pores, whether they are distant or jumpy or grateful if you touch them – you can feel gratefulness because you can literally feel a sense of them melting. When working with elderly people, especially single ones, it is often good to touch their head or face if you can, for example in the process of healing. They may not have felt a kind touch in that sensitive area for a very long time. Head massage is amazing for melting tension, and communicating empathy. Obviously your intention is communicated to them in the touch as well, so you'd better have good intentions.

We are multifaceted beings and I observe that all our senses are multidimensional if we are open enough to them, and more so if we don't abuse them through brash living. This has really made me wonder if ESP is actually a phenomenon in itself or if everything is just an extension of our usual senses. I think it is perhaps just a finer level of existing senses, and we can all learn to use them to this degree. It is just a matter of giving it enough attention, of noticing details, learning and becoming more confident as we see that what we perceive does actually turn out to be correct, or useful. Intuition is perhaps just that ability to be aware enough and to trust your senses.

Often things are communicated to us in symbols and we somehow understand them, as they seem to be in the global subconscious, transcending all boundaries of time, place, and language limits. Abstract artists, poets, and songwriters can use these to communicate things in a way that leaves room for individual interpretation, so it is much more powerful, for example, than using didactic language that tries to tell you what to think and do instead of showing you an idea and allowing you to develop your own response. This is particularly good for certain topics. Surreal writing or art seems to me to come in a raw and rich organic form via several of your senses, so it feels more as if you are getting the original information for yourself, instead of the flatness of the didactic which only leaves room for agreement or rejection. It gives you a whole new discovery to interpret and consider.

In his book on Shamanism – Roger Walsh says that the **Buddhist altered state of examining detail and of breaking things down**, even the ego, into microscopic dissections, is different. However, although there seems to be no recording of Shamans using this sort of state, I don't see why they might not have done so. I can imagine a Shaman sitting watching the community around him and seeing all the tiny motivations behind every move and laughing to himself. He would keep this private though, not talk about it, as he would be maintaining his place of power and respect in the community through a projected ego or persona. This need not be an ego he actually felt, as in how we would describe an egotistical person, but it would be a tool that he used as necessary, to set himself apart in his role.

I also enjoy the objective state of sitting watching people go by sometimes, observing human nature, and I love stories that include a detailed understanding of human nature too, depicting humanity in a gently honest way, as opposed to meaningless lists of what a person is wearing or doing.

The yogic state of pure consciousness is something I often enjoy, and I have no reason to believe that Shamans could not have done so. However there would have been a bit of a contradiction between their journey work based on a cosmic map stemming from cultural belief, and the blissful state that opens you wide to a unified oneness. How could such intricate maps and detailed beliefs exist alongside this unity? Yet, there is no reason why one could not use them at certain levels for certain purposes, and still go beyond them at other times. So, did the practitioner believe exclusively in their cultural system, or did he or she see it as a construct to achieve certain objectives, as we can now?

Perhaps there are layers within layers when it comes to our consciousness. Many of my experiences might suggest this, just like the levels of our auras which reflect the stepping down of pure energy to the physically manifest body. Different states of consciousness may progress from an inner circle to ever expanding outer circles, like some of Ken Wilber's diagrams suggest. I myself have used journeying as an early level of exploration, and can teach others to do so, but also to go way beyond this. Perhaps there is no paradox between states where we feel at least partially separate, and states where we feel at one with everything, between duality and non-duality, perhaps they are just different parts of the same overall journey.

Roger Walsh also says that speaking in the yogic state of blissful oneness may break their intense concentration. Again I argue that concentration should never be that intense, it should be soft! Yes, I agree, it is preferable not to have to speak or be interrupted when in such a deep state, but I find that it is still possible to maintain it in all sorts of situations, including walking about and doing certain things, or even waiting in a post office queue or a traffic jam. If in a difficult situation I find the following phrase a good one to open the focus, the gate to blissfulness: "I love and am loved" – referring to my relationship with the universe. It can also be useful to focus on the breath. Roger Walsh says that attention is fixed inwardly, but I find that it is a union of the inner and the outer, which can be quickly accentuated through intention. I feel as though I go beyond time, space, or any other limitation, and experience a state of union with the entire universe, which I feel both within me and all around me, even beyond that, not being limited to anything at all.

I was pleased to find that Abraham Maslow (previously discussed) **also found in his explorations that he kept having to deconstruct old ideas and concepts as he progressed, including perpetually coping with seeming paradoxes.**

This collapse of paradoxes, which is fundamental to my book, is similar to the whole state of higher consciousness – things break down yes, but it is not a destructive breaking down, and does not feel like a loss of anything. It is a melding of everything into a beautiful overall oneness, an understanding of how each paradox melts away to show that it was only a construct in the first place. We can see how we have to live with the system of paradoxes to be able to cope on this planet. We need some sort of system or web of ideas to base our lives on, before we can learn to also see beyond it to something else. It is kind of like we forgot how things were on earth and had to learn all over again. (Except that I remembered as a very young child, knowing some of these things, so I guess I was lucky enough to have a bit of a head start, or perhaps we all retain a glimpse of this as children, then lose it as we get caught up in the systems imposed on us.)

The system is still good for some things, to be able to exist alongside our fellows in a world of jobs and property etc, but once we understand that it is only an artificially constructed reality (kind of like the shaman's cultural map), we can step outside of it whenever it is useful to do so, and observe it objectively.

One then realises that if we have constructed such things from our consciousness, then we must really be able to construct whatever we choose to. We could change things to make them work better.

Time is a funny thing! While I know it is not strictly linear – and that in a sense I have all the time I need – I also know that I must focus on the present when I am dowsing for what is happening in the earth for example, or I may get readings about water that was there before. Although it's now dried up, there's still an imprint. Looking for a lost animal or person is difficult if they keep moving, as you get readings from every bit of their trail. I guess it works in the same terms that we can understand time in, so we need to ask questions that enable us to be clear about the answers. I can't seem to divine into the future – but I think that may be to do with my belief that it probably isn't right to do so. I do occasionally pick up tiny bits unbidden, especially when only a couple of minutes ahead, as in a warning (letting me know to drive round a corner very slowly as there is someone parked there with a car door open, or telling me that someone is about to arrive or phone, for example). Perhaps these things are easier to pick up as they are already in the process of happening. It's not the actual grabbing of the phone, it's the thought of doing it that triggers the connection. (Our cats often come to meet us half way when they feel us decide to head home.) Some things that happen quite far ahead seem easier for some people to pick up for example if they are about large disasters, almost as if there is a backwards flowing shockwave.

Nihilism in relation to time

There is a huge difficulty when discussing time, or whether things are preordained or not. If you believe that everything is predestined then it would be easy to be nihilistic. If everything is set out already then what would be the point of us learning, striving, doing anything much at all with our lives? I don't think that can truly be the case – or if it is – then it is still a vast multiple choice thing where the outcomes are one of millions, depending on each choice we make along the way.

I think pretty much all the great poets, artists, philosophers, musicians…. Have been through the grey tunnel of nihilism, struggling with these concepts, but most of them come out of the other end. I think that this can also be a part of growing up, going through the teenage years etc, especially if there is not much else to focus on. There is little sense of having to pull together, not much positive sense of identity, instead there are disappointments – families splitting up, or being pulled apart by war, or maybe having to move for jobs (so less support from grandparents to help bring up children), no sense of being part of a team (unless you join some organisation), no huge hope for meaningful jobs even if you study hard. You just have to somehow keep trying at life in a background of economic and political failure and deception, knowing how badly we damage our planet and each other when we get things wrong, trying to find something to hold on to that won't break. At the end of the day, despite maybe finding some good friends or mentors, we have to rely on ourselves and our tentative connection to the imperative of life. (Even though I was extremely lucky to grow up in idyllic natural surroundings, from about 9 onwards I suffered agonies over the appalling things humans can do to each other and the planet, and tried to shoot myself while still in junior school, where I didn't fit in well. I did better a little while after starting boarding high school. I found adult mentors and loads of good stuff to do, plus ways of getting on socially.) There *is* good stuff going on you could join in with, or you could start something to suit you.

I do believe that we are here for a purpose, but that purpose is not fixed, it's up to us to find what fits with us. We've come into a certain set of circumstances, and a lot depends on our response to them. The choices we make may need revising if our understanding of things changes as we go. We should not be afraid of making mistakes, we can always learn from them, and sometimes we would never have found our answers if we hadn't tried something else first.

The holy grail is a symbol of what can be discovered within each of us, but we may have to clean off a fair bit of gunk, mostly dumped on us by other people, to be able to drink from it. It also helps to have a sense of humour to enable us to look at things in different ways. **Humour loosens the grip of dirt,** it helps save us from turning to addictions to try to drown out our more sickening thoughts. Art helps us to work through pains that our artistic minds are sensitive to. Creativity leads us to examine our world in detail, with all its' pro's and con's, yet hopefully make something beautiful. It also enables us to communicate to others what we feel.

There seems to be an imperative to be in a process, to be constantly observing, learning & becoming. If we had finished doing that, or were only some puppet of pre-ordained circumstance, then I don't think we would be here at all.

Without the matrix of apparent opposites, there would probably not be life in the first place. How would we be alive if we were not able to DO things, therefore experience, or learn anything. Everything would the same! The matrix gives us a basis to begin from, to grow with, to become partly free of, but never entirely – as on the physical plane we cannot be totally free of it. Even if we are aware enough to be totally objective, we still depend on it for the world to function, just as we depend on our egos to function, even when we have coaxed them into their appropriate place so that they don't drive us, but we use them as tools. We also use our logical minds as tools once our deep spiritual or soulful mind rises to take its rightful place.

Our soulful mind is not just in our heads, it is everywhere. Our brains are just sets of receptors and processors really, and so are the neurones distributed around all the major organs of the body. We process things as individuals in a combination of ways, but we are also linked to vast amounts of information all around us, so we should accept that oneness and separateness each have their place – they are both true & useful if you use them alongside each other instead of trying to cling to one or the other.

When we meditate to become one with all consciousness, we can feel every cell in our bodies singing, resonating with the harmony of it. There is no sense of time at all. You could be in that state for a minute or an hour and you wouldn't truly know the difference until you look at something that gives you a clue, such as a clock, or the shadows that have grown long. I do however get a sense of FLOW. I conclude that our sense of time is very relative. When at one with the universe, time is in a sense meaningless because it is such an infinite state that our idea of time is inconsequential. The sense of flow that I get seems to indicate a timelessness itself; things change in cycles, yes, but they always exist – like tides in an ocean, perhaps an umbilical suck and pull between one universe and another even, the suck in and spewing out of a black hole, the compressing of sand into rock and the erosion of the rock into sand again, or like seasons where old things become new things – even compost being part of this. Water goes round in cycles between earth and air, air goes round in cycles between plants and animals (including humans), wind and currents continually circulate trying to rebalance pressures and temperatures. Fire is part of the death and rebirth of things too, from plants to planets.

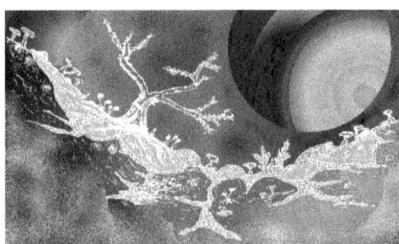

In the non-dual state of consciousness, as identified by Ken Wilber, we finally blend all the altered states of consciousness back into our 'normal' life – realizing that everything in our 'normal' life is a projection of our consciousness. **This is the objective state of which I speak,** where we are able to rise above the everyday stuff, see how & why people create & react to situations, understand that all of this also belongs to the oneness. So we are all interlinked & should not judge one thing from the other. If I judged someone or something then I would also be judging myself. Thus we learn to empathize through our understanding, and cease to be so reactive. In the objective state we can shrug, smile, say okay, and let it flow with no drama. We might even discover that things can work out advantageously after all.

If shamans did experience being at one with everything – then it would probably not have been recorded or passed on orally. Within their own circles they would have wanted those around them to focus on their power as beings apart, so that they would trust them as their shaman in times of need. Allowing westerners to learn their skills now, and laughing at them in a loving way might indicate that they do see the overall picture of unity, otherwise they might not have had the understanding to allow people from such differing backgrounds to attempt to learn their skills.

It is only when we have experienced opening to the bigger picture and the sense of unity, that we know that everything around us is only the little work of men superimposed on a greater canvas, and can laugh at ourselves and our little egos, with all their false strivings.

As for whether our consciousness evolves or not – as a species – or individually – I'm not so sure. If ancient civilizations had shamans who could do what we do now, then perhaps not, but perhaps we have added information & a wider variety of tools. Yet our tools can be used against us, so we have to be very aware to keep ahead. There is so much media manipulation going on….. just start looking out for it and you will see what I mean! We are fed propaganda to try to mask the truth, and told what to think about everything. We can use the internet to interact, to find out things, to organize ourselves, but even that is monitored. There is also a danger of us depending so much on our technology that we forget how to use our more natural tools. Children are born intuitive, but school and grown ups tend to suppress it. Machines can discover a lot about what is under the earth for example, but natural divination is still better, giving a much more detailed picture. Machines can even do things like sound healing, but intuitive sound healing is still much better. In any form of healing, our minds and bodies can cope with all the nuances and respond appropriately and effectively. Our intuition can pick up what is going on inside someone's body and make fine adjustments in the energy systems in an overall holistic way, to help the body heal any situation, even those caused by emotional or mental effects, not just physical.

If we evolve our consciousness individually then basically we start (in most of the modern world at least) with a person with an idea of being a separate mind – then eventually he discovers that this consciousness he has worked so hard to expand does not actually belong to him alone – it is part of a much greater whole. This may sound like a bitter joke, but actually it is a beautiful concept, as we realize that each one of us can help others come forward, as our consciousness provides an example to theirs, simply because they share space. People in a room can literally consent (without a need for words) to tune in together with their higher minds to achieve some purpose. People separated by physical distance can blend their higher minds too, and literally have a conversation, or heal one another, or agree to add their energy to some cause such as enhancing peace in any given situation.

If you observe a person in meditation who truly comes to the understanding for the first time of how we are all interlinked, you will see them smiling or hear them laughing out loud. They will have beautiful visions of the interlinking of all of life, because they realize then how enduring it all is, how indestructible consciousness and energy is, because they are the very source of everything. They will perceive the absolute joy of the flow emanating everywhere.

Although we are all interlinked, we still have the ability to greatly affect our individual experience and lives on this planet through what we choose to do with our discovery. It may seem to casual observers that we are the same person, but really we are very much changed, at peace with our responsibility of knowing what we know, doing what we do, being who we are.

So, being a spiritual 'master' can seem to mean being a master of nothing, but as always, beyond the supposed nothing, there is a whole array of possibility and fullness. You just let go of all the old unhelpful stuff and align yourself with the awesome pure energy of life.

Letting go means no longer trying to hold onto every little result of everything you try to do, as you know now that everything you do counts in a much deeper way, and is part of the flow of life. It all works so much better if you tune into the bigger picture, rather than to try to fiddle endlessly with all the details to manipulate results (including how people think and react). You know that if your overall intention is good, and clear, then you will be much more likely to get on well with things, and the little details will almost take care of themselves. You cease to waste energy where it's not needed, and stop getting in your own way. You are more relaxed and people like you better, and things tend to almost fall into place.

Accessing evolved states of consciousness enables us to do unusual things, access special information, heal etc. We are enabled to live our lives in a self-actualized state, no longer being tossed about by the vagaries of wayward emotional reactions (of ourselves and others), but responding in a steadfast way. We can make choices based upon an overall enlightened picture rather than trying to make sense of a mass of confused perceptions. We can be a small example, perhaps even helping others to reach more enlightened states more easily, and thus raising the level of thinking generally, so that more people may wish with specific intent for peace and goodwill.

I'm not sure if at the end of the day this gets us anywhere better in the long run – as history shows, there are always those who misuse any kind of power – and it seems as if this may have as often as not caused the downfall of civilizations…. But it certainly makes me feel a lot better about how I am living in the meantime.

Perhaps life will always return to its cycles – starting again after every disaster, rising and falling throughout 'time', just like anything else, one huge infinite multidimensional wave pattern, or cycle of sucking in and pouring outwards, like a huge creative breathing cycle. Waves, particles, fractals – you see them everywhere in nature, in star systems, and in our own bodies. The suck and pull I sense at the base of life could be the Involution from pure spirit to physicality (and forgetfulness), and the Evolution of awareness and consciousness (remembering of our true nature).

As we have seen, there are no real paradoxes. Nothing is ever bad or good, (or in fact any of the other supposed opposites), all is part of the same thing, and each is simply representative of what stage of development we are at. (The supposed paradoxes simply show us what we are still learning.)

"The void folds, enfolds, and outfolds potentialities." – and "particles don't travel – they appear and reappear." Said David Bohm.

"Heaven, earth, and the ten thousand things form one body". said Confucius.

There must be a lot of frustrated historians out there, starting out as students discovering what happened as if it were all new, but then seeing how we repeat the old mistakes. Our foray into altered states of consciousness is similar, it is so exciting when we first discover our huge potential, finding out things about ourselves anew, even about life and death, yet so many have done it all before…… and humanity continues to wage unjust wars, destroy cultures, denude rainforests, wreak havoc….. and the 'powerful' few have too much control, having devised bogus systems and used us like pawns in a chess game.

Zen and other mystical traditions suggest that "The 'I', one's real and most intimate self, pervades the universe and all other beings". (All the other 'I's must pervade both us and the universe too.)

Buddha says **"See yourself in others. Then whom can you hurt? What harm can you do?"** Can we all evolve enough to stop hurting & harming others, and thus ourselves? I think that the more of us who try, the more likely we are to enable others to try too.

I think that this is the only way for the human race to have a chance of surviving. Arguing over policies & resources, etc, can't lead us out of the quagmire per se; although of course we do need to make our views heard and help make a difference. Ideally though, we all need to be fully conscious to be able to deal with things properly, including the tricky ones who have very different agendas, suppressing useful advancements, wanting control of the masses, even to reduce their numbers, not caring about wreaking havoc on lives & places so that they can keep taking for themselves. Perhaps we can stop this, but we have to come up with alternative ways of living so that we can reject their unfair systems. These are only constructs that can be changed.

Perhaps we will be able to break through more into the NEW, instead of just repeating the old ideas amassed in the collective unconscious. We need to fly out of boxes and beyond limited ideas, perhaps setting our logical minds aside temporarily to reach our epiphany, then letting them back in to plan practical details.

Ramtha said in "A Beginners Guide to Creating Reality":
"Consciousness and Energy Create Reality", and "Our purpose is to make known the unknown". Also, the "Soul is the recorder of all experience and the wisdom gained in the journey of involution and evolution." And "Consciousness has no laws…. It has free rein. Energy is the handmaiden of thoughts. It is what collapses the subatomic world into particle reality and creates magnetic fields to draw what is already known into your hands."

Meister Eckhart said **"The whole scattered world of lower things is gathered up to oneness when the soul climbs up to that life in which there are no opposites."**

Ideas and more quotations to think about:

* Expanding Time (or contracting it) – Instead of panicking if one is running out of time, get into the zone, and ask the universe for it to be expanded to allow you to cope, and one way or another you will manage much better.
* Step into Seed Power – your Soul's Intention in this life. Identify with it as part of your core identity, smile often when you think of it, and it will flow towards your good energy.
* List your gifts of grace – your natural skills that help you fulfil your intention, remind yourself of them, and be grateful for them. This will help keep you positive and on track.
* Exist with a foot in both worlds. Remember, you create your own reality, but you also have to live alongside other people's realities. Try to consider their position and not judge them. Also you have different parts of yourself that show up in different circumstances, for example: the dancer, the healer, the worker, etc, etc …. Sometimes these may seem to be in conflict with each other – one could take itself very seriously and the other be so chilled out that they don't agree – but there is no reason at all why they should not all exist in balance within you. Again, don't judge, allow yourself to be as you are. All the other parts of you such as your ego, and your spiritual side, also need to co-exist. You need each part for different aspects of your life. You cannot be fully in one or the other all the time. After a very focused day you may need to just chill out by doing something that does not require you to think too much, and always you need sufficient sleep and optimum nutrition to recharge. Flow between the different states

as needed – it is a natural process of life. Don't expect yourself to be permanently in the zone or wide awake!

* Energy management – In my late teens and early twenties I used to have periods where I would not sleep or eat much as I was busy writing or painting, but then the inevitable exhaustion would set in (mental and physical, so also causing depression), so I learnt to plan to manage my energy better. Obviously you need to first be aware of what you need to manage, and the body is very good at giving us the signs, for example – pain shows something that needs attention, so it is no good just taking loads of painkillers. (If you take painkillers for long periods the body actually increases your ability to feel pain so that you will stop ignoring the message!) It is always best to listen to your body's needs, and to balance activities with rest and exercise and good food. (Our needs are quite individual so find out what suits you best.)

* Security – You need to feel secure about your identity as an individual before you can fully relax into a feeling of oneness with everything. If you are not, then you might have a bit of an issue with your ego being too afraid to let you transcend it. It makes sense that it would be concerned about possibly losing your grounding in the world, so don't be impatient with it, just try to let it know that it's okay, by embracing all that you are.

* Interim challenges to build your strength, and fire to temper your gold (rites of passage, or quests) – something like walking the Inca Trail, or anything you might want to do, but also see as a bit of a challenge, is probably very good for you. We even tend to learn through hardship, so try to bear this in mind when things seem difficult. Look for the lesson, or test, and remember that there are usually others struggling even more in comparison.

Meister Eckhart also said that the soul is generative in nature – it has the power to create form out of the intention which is encoded within its very substance. We need to discover our unique master intention and align ourselves with the sacred architecture of our own soul. You can usually find this if you follow your heart instead of the vagaries of the mind and ego, which tend to try to seek gratification in pleasing others and collecting ultimately meaningless things and/or accolades. Of course you can be kind to others, and progress in a job, as well as following your soul path, they don't have to be mutually exclusive so long as one doesn't obscure the other. Look at what your best skills are and what you most love doing, as they are usually part of your gift and soul purpose.

* You can use pictures, symbols, and songs or poems to express and enhance your intended journey-path. You can ask the universe to show you helpers to guide you in carrying out your intention.
* Give gifts to your helpers – sunbeam, flower etc. Ask advice anytime.
* Walk on the wild side. Don't be afraid to enjoy life, and to connect with the Spirits of Place, the Sacredness of Plants, Animals, the Elements, and Silence. Be centred (balanced and grounded) and pour forth the abundance of your being.
* Seek your Core Purpose for being here, and feel its echoes everywhere. Find the seat of joy in your body and expand it, more, more. Smile or laugh as you connect with it.
* Feel the fire of creation – it is like a primordial love affair – an invisible torrent. Feel its spiralling energy throughout the universe connecting with your own creative energy. Connect your physical energy to the mental energy of inspiration. Dance and dream the seed of whatever you want to be, do, or create.
* Cycles of becoming – be aware that things rise and fall – this is all very natural – progression, then a bit of a fall back, or a test, then more progression. Don't allow setbacks to stop you, just go forward again when you are ready. Also bear in mind that sometimes we need a break to assimilate information or process change.
* Don't fear transformation – you have NOTHING to lose.
* You could try Time Diving – imagine going through a gateway into the depths of yourself, or your idea, to explore possibilities, and peek at what something might look like once you have got it to a certain stage.
* You could imagine crossing time and dimensions to seek another version of yourself that has taken different choices in life, and so can offer to share their experiences or knowledge of their areas of expertise. You first need to know what sort of advice you are looking for and then find the right version of yourself to offer it. Meditate upon your intention then take your leap to meet this other self.
* Freedom is "the vehicle to travel to the ends of the universe in, and celebrate the sheer exuberance of being….." You are free when you allow your mind to be so.

* Again in meditation, you could imagine a Journey either to the Quantum Vacuum or to the Light, and ask the purpose of creation (and of all the myriad forms).
* When you are aligned with the universe and all creation, you can feel this – "I am no thing, yet from my boundless emptiness all things arise. Out of me, light is born, galaxies, elements, birds, rocks, the sea, bacteria to live in the soil……..." Feel the light in your body as the energy connects and rises.
* Shaping Matter & the way things work – we are deeply embedded in the web of life which we ourselves help weave. Consciousness shapes matter, and we can redirect the future of our planet. We do not have to submit to imposed systems, we can speak out and find, or even invent ways of doing things differently.
* Each of us has our unique place within the evolving universe – we should honour that.
* What is the purpose of the planet? Your role? Let it all unfold.
* Feel the Love & give a prayer of thanks and grace.
* Beginnings & endings – are all part of the same journey.

"To pay attention, this is our endless and proper work." From the wonderful poet, Mary Oliver.

I believe that to be conscious, even just a little bit, means that we are paying attention to everything around us, witnessing things, experiencing life, and being the person we choose to be. Of course, the more consciously we do that the more we will notice and learn, and the more that will inform and enrich our experience of life, in turn expanding our consciousness further. So as our consciousness expands more, we are able to choose more accurately who we are being exactly, and thus also feel more confident in having a say in things that affect how we want to live our lives, and how we think the world should be.

The Fragility and Susceptibility of what we might call 'Reality'

Look everywhere. There are miracles and curiosities to fascinate and intrigue for many lifetimes. The intricacies of nature and everything in the world and universe around us from the miniscule to the infinite; physical, chemical and biological functionality; consciousness, intelligence and the ability to learn; evolution, and the imperative for life; beauty and other abstract interpretations; language and other forms of communication; how we make our way here and develop social patterns of culture and meaningfulness; how we organize ourselves and others; moral imperatives; the practicalities of survival and all the embellishments we pile on top; thought, beliefs, logic, intuition, ideas; inventing, creating, information, knowledge; emotions, sensations, experience, behaviour.

We are each unique individuals arising from a combination of genetic, inherited, and learned information, all of which can be extremely fallible. Things taught to us when we are young are quite deeply ingrained. Obviously some of it (like don't stick your finger in a wall socket) is very useful, but some of it is only opinion – an amalgamation of views from people you just happen to have had contact with. A bit later on we have access to lots of other information via books, media, internet etc, but it is important to remember that most of this is still just opinion, and can often be biased. Even subjects such as history and religion are presented according to the government's or presenter's or author's point of view. Science is continually changing. Newspapers and TV channels tend to cover news in the way that is most useful to them (and those who fund them). Research is also subject to the decisions of those who fund projects, and can be distorted by business interests. Pretty much anyone can say what they want on the internet, so our powers of discernment need to be used to a great degree there too.

Not one of us can have a completely objective view as we can't access and filter all knowledge available, so we must accept that our views are bound to be subjective   Our understanding and responses are all very personal, and our views extremely varied. We tend to make each new thing fit in with the picture we have already started in our heads, but we often have to go back and adjust the picture if we want to be honest about our view of reality as we continually expand it. We are taking in vast amounts of information from others all the time, so need to ensure we are processing that to develop our own true reflection of who we are.

    We need to trust our own intuition in life, and also not be afraid to play with it, let it guide our creativity, use our minds to create whatever helps us, even if they seem like wild imaginings sometimes.

    As Max Planck said "When you change the way you look at things, the things you look at change."

MOTIVE (Motif)

Lured, enticed, intrigued;
always becoming the person I am
about to know even better than the one before.

Called by the spirits of water,
sun, wind, earth and rock, plants – to feel
the intricate web of sights,
sounds, scents, sensations – wrapped all around;
and within, the web that forms the world,
but that still has gaps we can see through to others,
and twists we can travel back-to-front or inside-out in.

Reading messages, listening to patterns,
absorbing power and love, being given true gifts.
Being a part of all uniqueness
stemming from one consciousness.

Respectfully observing, witnessing what is real
but can always be changed
in the timing of vibrations, or sequence of thoughts,
or tweak of the grid pattern, reframing;
in the quality of light, the touch of heat or cold,
the flight of colours.

Slowly, yet quickly, I walk my path of heart
which keeps me safe and confident,
being consumed only by the urge to learn more,
yet filled with peace and joy.

I see flowers bursting from muscles and minds,
pigeons taking flight from roofs of cars

and heading off into bushes at the left of the road.
I see squiggles of energy wavering,
where before there were only solid lines.
Meanings of objects take on different significances
when their molecular structures scramble before your eyes.
Nothing is well defined, the flow blurs
as we learn to swim.

We make the vision happen,
just as we dream we want it to begin,
and only we can laugh
as we try to grasp the responsibility
for all futures and pasts
dancing right now in multi-directions.

Some possible Waking Dream tricks to play with:

Freedom Zoning or Hyper-Dreaming

This is a technique where your mind is set free to range over ideas and zone in on areas of particular interest to explore possibilities / ask questions, like dreaming an experience, though awake. You might want to do this to help you decide on whether to go forward with an idea or not, or to imagine you have taken a leap forwards and then work out what you have done and how, to help give you ideas.

    For example we could create a meditation which will set your mind going into this relaxed but active state where it is like flying around in a way that it can see everything, it is like an aerial view but you see through things, and you can also tilt the perspective to get a better idea of proportions, or better views of details.

    Then you are led by tasks / questions (such as – "now find a patch in the future, say about 5 years ahead, where you can see yourself doing something you really want to do"). Then you can go into more specifics like asking what they are doing, asking if they are enjoying it, asking how they manage to do such a task, ask if they have trained for it, ask if they have natural ability for it, ask if it feels good in their hearts to do it, and why.

    So you could use this to explore future options. A person may find out that something they thought they might like is something they actually find boring or difficult, thus avoid wasting the years finding that out via actual experience.

They might also use it to resolve problems, for example they could try out different scenarios to see if they work or not, see other people's reactions, see results, all without them being real as yet, so saving mistakes, and finding useful solutions. It's a lot more than thinking something through logically, it is a realistic experience of that future scenario through a waking dream state.

Or they might find an answer for example, that if they speak to certain people this might lead to a certain job.

Remember to view details such as expressions, colours, sense emotions, count things, check times, names, dates where appropriate.

You can also use this technique to have a difficult conversation with someone for example forgiving your parents or apologizing to your husband/wife or a friend. If you imagine the process effectively, it is almost as if it actually happened! It is possible that your higher self reached the higher self of the other and actually communicated something, but even if that is not the case, this still makes a difference. All the emotive tension has gone out of you, and it is then so much easier to actually do it with the person, or in fact you may not even need to do it as you will act as if you have already done it and the other person will pick up on that, will respond to your new attitude, and things may be just fine from there on in. Sometimes, for example if forgiving things from way back in the past, it may indeed be better not to bring it up again with the other person, but just to deal with it in this way, releasing your own tensions about it.

You can also meet other versions of yourself – ones who made different choices, learnt different things. Ask to meet a version who has the skills or knowledge you seek, and ask them to teach you. Some people call this "quantum jumping".

Shamanic Dreaming (note – without the use of drugs)

I have discussed this before but just wanted to bring it in here as a reminder and to contrast it with these other ideas. This concentrates on dream-journeying in the natural world of places, plants, and animals. However it can also bring you answers to many things meaningful to your own (or another's) life, as well as to the traditional queries about why someone is ill and what can be done to help. It allows access to surprisingly deep knowledge.

Infinity Dreaming

Here you can meditate on a sort of space we might call – whatever you like – but actually it could be a unique universe – and just let our minds range free there to see what this might mean to us.

You might experience visions that come from within as well as from the wider universe because it is all connected.

Can you imagine infinity? How would you relate the concept of it?

There has been much mention of our universe expanding….. so what is it expanding into? Is it just nothingness? If it's still expanding then how can it already be infinite, and then be more infinite?

Could there maybe be universes upon universes within each other? They might be bubbles inside of each other, or they may exist in different dimensional spaces, all sort of multiplied on top of each other. There may be stuff like that all around us right now!

If we are part of a stream of consciousness then surely that stream is everywhere, inside of us and outside of us, and in all conceivable (and even inconceivable) spaces?

Why not try to meditate on this, see what visions you can come up with. Just let you mind go, it is pretty amazing what it can do if you let it.

It can be great fun to write down or draw what you experience.

Cosmic Dreaming

I previously touched on this idea of the cosmos having its own dream of everything that might be possible. (After all it is continuing to create us, and a whole host of things. Many of its creations also create too.)

This would be great to tune into instead of the collective unconscious (ref Jung), which is limited to the past ideas and experiences of man and the earth, and therefore cannot take us forwards to new imaginings. (The clue is in the word – unconscious – it's a random heap of stuff!) It is good to access for Diviners needing knowledge of what exists in certain places now (water, minerals, etc), or of what has happened in the past (in a crime for instance). However, when we want to envisage new possibilities, then Cosmic Dreaming can help you fly right outside of any boxes or other limitations that your mind might try to impose. We set logic aside, have our visions, then can often see (or work out) the actual logic afterwards. (Many scientists have done this when making a breakthrough.) It's different from infinity dreaming, which is exploring the vastness around us, as us, a small part of it looking outwards. Cosmic dreaming is like trying to get inside the mind of God or the original source of all creation / consciousness, and see how things work from that perspective, whether it is random, or all unfolds according to certain patterns, for example, or whether there is actual direction to it or not.

We can then relate this to our own selves and our abilities to dream our existence.

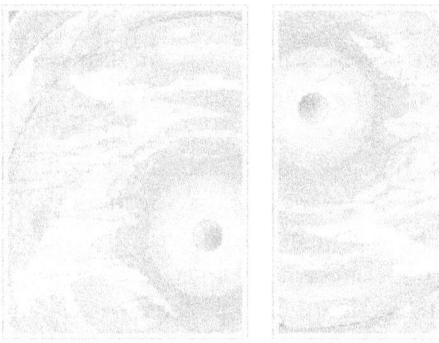

FLOW – Abundance of life, and power of selfhood.
A stream of consciousness piece….

Life streams
out of everything
into everything,
free to come and go,
never ending,
simply moving on,
breathing everywhere.

Bags of life

of all types, bursting,
streaming, filled,
easing or spicing time.

Litheness of snakes,
playfulness of cats,
freedom of birds in flight,
emerging shadow sides,
all kinds of totems, myths.

I am safe
no matter what
animal comes out
from sky or bush -
I dance with it
in love
for life is various,
needing all.

It is not hungry enough
for human flesh,
or angry enough
to bite or claw.

Finding, observing, reframing
flowing words, recording thoughts –
everything really,
even the stupid and the fake
because they are funny,
not just sad.
Always the glad,
the flippant, the mad,
the gregarious, the gracious,
the silent lights flickering.

Watching
is life witnessing life,
remembering
how energy divides,
fascinated

by all its different dreams,
experiments of being.

Truth is what is
for you each second
slipping in and out
like breath, like dreams,
like patiently being.

Sacred moments from past lives
become fluid in this
passing through to the next
as we walk down the street
talking about conspiracies
we have known, forgotten, remembered,
just like ourselves
walking down the street
yesterday, beyond –
here tentatively existing
as energy arising into this form
from other forms, and into more,
not mattering, except to continue,
somewhere expressing itself,
becoming what it is
you think
everyday moving with change
so that what you think
can twist.

We know and we don't know
all at the same time.
We live in two worlds
existing in the dream of others
ss well as in our own,
doing things we don't want to do
as well as those we do,
trying to see objectively
while being submerged;

But we can swim

with our heads above water,
kicking and flailing maybe,
but moving forwards

like a flower in love

we need the sun and water
and air and earth
so that we can be whole.

Our earth sustains us,
being part of us,
joined like lovers
subconsciously
as we feel each other
existing within ourselves,
dreaming that being is solid
instead of like passing kisses of angels
before they plummet into flames,
burning yet rising again
to writhe like snakes up into the air
so that they can re-emerge
in some other world,
flying free for observers not like ourselves
but who dream of us breathing
feeling us in sleep
as we feel them lurking in forests,
strange insects
dancing secretly nearer
behind us, underneath us
while all around us life is flourishing,
experience becoming
new imagined places for living.

Under the skin
the sameness and differences
merge as workings of biology.

Inside the earth
and outside the planet's orbit

energy teems.

We feel it burning coldly,
softly intriguing
thrumming like melodious pianos
slowly shifting keys
while life transforms itself.
The previously existing life
and the new forms witness each other,
becoming endlessly more and more -
fractal patterns shooting off
in all directions at once,
intricate spirals weaving,
atomic mirroring,
clouds swelling, billowing.

Life excessive
as it knows no other way
but to spread and add to and change
its own essence.

Each choosing
agrees with itself,
cannot help but agree with the whole.
Oneness consists of diversity
adding up, it cannot be anything less;
so choose as much as you want
and feel the glee of it
agreeing with all other agreements
to be one!

Where do your ideas
of yourself come from
but from the million choices
being spread around the universe
from this and other worlds.

You are being
the seed of new born old
to become part of the mulch

nourishing all species.

Swamp of ideas
mixing remnants of existence
like witch brews
to make something new
to give back to the warm heart.

Liquid wisdom again
breeding more of itself
but losing part of the story
only to find it looking out at us
from the face of mars or the moon
one night cold and alone,
not knowing that separation is the biggest lie,
as we don't see each other
looking in the same mirror at different times,
until we compare notes
or re-connect with the collective dreaming
spreading always out.

Talking is the sound
of the one mother within us
trying to become loud
in its asking for forgiveness
and recognition
and sweet milk too.

Singing is the burnt angel
recycling its life through all of us,
calling to other universes
to join in with our love.

Seething space
full of all the girls dancing
rhythms of circling
flowing colours
out there in the dark
to attract men.

We seek
answers, anything,
when really our language
and understanding
is never enough
to cope with the fullness

unless you understand
that emptiness becomes fullness
all by itself
if you switch your brain off.

We wake up
and everything is different
even though we pretend it's the same,
but our eyes reflect
the newness of this day
that can never be as before
the way we accelerate
from our beds out into the universe.

We are welcomed
no matter how naughty we have been.
Destruction happens
but life goes on
because energy cannot die,
so you and I
can go on loving forever.

If we are conscious enough
to recognise ourselves and each other
in everything around us,
then we have won the long dream
(longer than any power planned histories
or blatant economic tricks).

Consciousness itself has
become unlimited
simply because we know that we are.
Harmony across the abyss

is always possible if we live like this,
recognising the closeness of distance
holding us yet not holding.

Enfolding us
in its warm wide embrace,
the universe whispers to us,
infinitely wise,
always giving us what we need
simply because we accept.

What you and I need
is nothing more than trust.
We know what lies between
us and the sea.
We know how gladness
is like a tide coming in,
and how the little creatures weave
their bubbles in the sand.

Flowers fall on the earth
as we pass with heads bowed,
going towards our centre.

At long last
we are devoured,
our egos step aside,
surrendering to the path.

Our feet take us to the edge
where wind whips in our hair,
blowing away remaining dregs
so that we can see clearly.

The beacon
that is me to you
and you to me
flies in our foreheads
hot and excited
yet beautifully cool.

Put your lips
on the rim of your own deceit
but don't drink the poison,
just spit it somewhere harmless
so it can help make new planets
out there in the darkness.

Even the black
gives rise to light eventually,
when the stuff in there burns itself out
through intense pressure,
the flare is again a beacon
to spark more life to begin.

What stays behind
is the deep cells inside
which divide as always once more
to reform life, attracting
in many different forms,
artistically portraying itself
across the canvas of earth and sky,
inside water, air, and even fire,
knowing more ways to fulfil its desire
than any of us can imagine.

I am ruthless in my own kingdom,
where even crocodiles wear smiles,
where even the enemy praises talent,
where mocking crowds disperse
with downcast eyes when needed,
where all ideas can be conceived
to play games with myself and my poems,
to trick my mind with my steady heart,
to keep awake through any drought.

We seeded the need for opposites
to define each other,
to experience emotions,
reactions; to learn,

to rise above these,
to enable us to recognise anything
as temporarily separate,
as aspects of ourselves reflecting
the variousness around us.

How else could we be
without a space to exist in,
a manufactured bubble,
an illusion, allowing us to create
our own dreams within the dream?

We have to slide in and out
of all realities simultaneously,
and off into the otherness
whenever we need to just be
ourselves, or replenished,
like children needing food.

What is the mood but every mood
upon us in this life of theatre
where the depths increase within,
where soft centres have tough exteriors?

We make and remake our own beds
and let the river flow over.

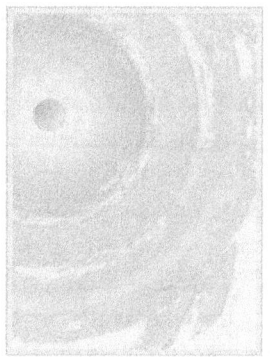

The Possibility of Consciously Evolving Consciousness.

There can surely be no doubt that our states of consciousness generally have evolved as a species. Apart from actual physical developments of the brain and our ability to think, we have learnt so many new things, can do so much, can travel so far and meet so many new people to interact with and learn from, have so many gadgets & other inventions. Yet still we seem stuck – some people would appear to be way behind others in their appreciation of the possibilities. The human race in general seems pretty bad at communication too. We often seem to react like toddlers having a tantrum or adolescents sulking, both individually and collectively (as nations for example). Can we trust our leaders, or ourselves, to do better?

    Far too often we have been taken advantage of by those with the power to pull the wool over our eyes. The evidence is out there, but we have been deliberately duped so that many of us either don't notice or don't react to what has been happening, perhaps believing we still need our current systems despite everything. However, in our information age, there should be no excuse for this…. We really should wake up and take notice of what is going on, and take responsibility for ending all the manipulation, and ensuring the survival of both ourselves and our world.

A word on distracting ourselves from our journeys:

Our minds throw up all sorts of defences to stop us engaging properly with ourselves, others, the world – because of our fear of what might happen. We rush around doing things to avoid acknowledging pain, for example, sadness at the loss of past relationships – to avoid facing it, and what it really means. This is dangerous to ourselves, and others, because it makes us likely to plunge into new relationships, or plans, or systems, without having much idea of what we are doing.

    In fact by dropping our defences we actually become more real. We acknowledge ourselves, others, the world – and give ourselves space to just be, to work through emotions, find understandings, and heal. (Instead of storing them up like ticking time-bombs to either explode later, or make us ill.)

    Fear also often prevents us from taking up new challenges such as a job we may love, or a scheme to change a situation, and we are very good at unconsciously sabotaging our own efforts. If we learn to trust ourselves, the possibilities are endless.

Of course we also distract ourselves terribly with things like TV, needless consumerism, drink, etc, etc.... all of which feeds us lots of unreal stuff to suppress the real, and shut off thinking / feeling, as well as interfering with our access to the truth of things going on around us.

Always you have to feel a thing properly to make your judgement of it go away .... Emotion, your body, the earth, a situation. When you become fully aware of something, you can see that it can no longer have any power over you through your irrational reactions to it. Once you know your feelings, your body, nature, you can surrender to a sense of things being connected and perfect just as they are. You let go of any concerns over them to enjoy instead an understanding of them. You become objective enough to exercise simple choice.

You accept the way your past feelings have made you the person you are, but now you are aware of that, you have the power to change anything you want. Some things can't be changed themselves, but our views of them can be. You accept the scars on your leg as being part of you, thus allowing others to accept them. So you learn to love your body just as it is. You have the power to choose whether to cover it up or not. Without emotional reactions colouring your decisions, you appreciate that your body still allows you to function beautifully. You enjoy your own slow breathing as you walk to work, you enjoy the scent of the flowers you pass instead of focusing angrily on the litter in the streets. You enjoy the touch of skin on skin as you have a massage.

You learn to navigate your own deepening path to knowing yourself and the world. You have dropped the smokescreen and the mind chatter that used to stop you from just being. Now you are opening to your ability to engage creatively with life in a non self-conscious and non-judgemental way. This gives you a sense of ease and freedom, and you can pass that feeling on by giving others the space and respect to find their own way.

Meditation is not a tool to control your minds, or suppress thoughts. It is a tool to transform your whole inner and outer ability to cope with life the way it is. It opens you to being able to engage with the flow effectively instead of cutting you off from it!

If one reaches similar conclusions to myself: that all the supposed opposites are not really opposites at all, but just part of the oneness, yet appearing as opposites to enable us to experience life in the physical (and emotional); then one can rise above being totally subjected to that, and see things more objectively (see a bigger picture).

This means that you will have reached a dual state of awareness that allows you to watch yourself living in that matrix of supposed paradoxes, and yet at the same time step outside of it, at least partly detached from it, knowing now that there is more to us than that.

We are then less caught up in the artificial busy-ness & anxiety that is the preoccupation of life in the matrix, and much more serene.

If you are stuck in the matrix then it is my guess that you are probably doing at least one of these:

- rebelling against the sense of being caught in a trap
- succumbing to depression
- dulling your mind with over-use of:
    - alcohol
    - and/or other substances
    - and/or bad food
    - and/or TV soaps
    - and/or violent games and films
- keeping yourself too busy to think about it!
- or you might be too busy using it to build your ego or your fortune – neither of which will mean anything later on, as they are false personal goals – whereas outside the matrix it is about the holistic overall network of life.

In the subjective state your reality and my reality appear very different, because they are totally coloured by our upbringing, beliefs, ideas instilled by others, actions, reactions, experience, learning, viewpoints, etc.

In the objective state we are freed of the limitations of the matrix with all its false appearances. We are connected with the oneness from whence we all came, and thus are more aligned with each other. We can feel the simple beauty of the universe in our hearts, and we feel grounded upon our beautiful earth. We can begin to see that life and death (and all the fluctuations in-between) are just parts of an energetic cycle, and thus begin to lose our fears. We tend naturally to reconnect with the deepest parts of ourselves and follow our imperatives to be who we want to be and do what we really feel drawn to doing with our lives. We are then living in the natural flow, and are far less inclined to cling to false needs and securities, feeling instead more fulfilled within ourselves

Once you are aware of being able to watch yourself, then it is easier to change anything you want. You can do self-development, you can use your own mind as a tool to observe, analyse, and modify (even your subconscious). You can literally learn to consciously evolve your own consciousness. You can see what sort of things work or not, and do more of what works, and learn more about what proves useful.

Tools such as the internet allow us to learn a whole lot more about what is going on in our world – we never used to be able to access such vast amounts of information. There are those who believe that we can now, in one generation, re-live all the experiences of past generations. If we are no longer having to learn from (an unreliable) history, but experiencing everything first hand, then we ought to be able to evolve rapidly as a species, particularly with regard to our personal and collective states of consciousness.

Apart from the ideas I am putting forward in this book, there are also other states of consciousness that people have experimented with and learned from. All of these have in some way helped to progress the evolution of our consciousness in general. Obviously we can access information written by those who have experienced such methods, or we can try them for ourselves, but there is also the notion that everything that man has experienced is added to our collective sub-consciousness (ref Jung), and thus can affect us all (as the information is broadcast in dreams, and is often accessed by poets & artists). Once we become attuned to the universal flow of energy, we can pick up on any information out there, and add that to our learning.

When I first started writing this book I thought that most altered states of consciousness were much the same, however after further research, I had to conclude that they were not. There actually seem to be several different types of altered states. I think that I did not realise this initially because I seem to be able to move between several of them (meditation, divination, remote-viewing, channelling, shamanic questing, and healing) so easily that I had not perceived there to be any sort of boundary or real distinction.

We can also use meditation for 'subtle activism' – which sows thought seeds for peace, love, health, positive change, etc into the collective consciousness, with the idea that it will positively help more people to shift to those levels of consciousness. There are many groups of people involved in doing this around the world, including our own 'Back to The Garden' group. Studies have shown that crime levels are lower, for example, when such experiments are under way.

    I originally had 2 question & answer sections in this book, including some channelled ones, as these all seemed to me to be a part of our look at states of consciousness, as well as our philosophical look at what life might be about / how things might work; however these will now appear in one or more companion books. There are also many other books (mine and those of other writers) offering more tools to empower you on your journeys.

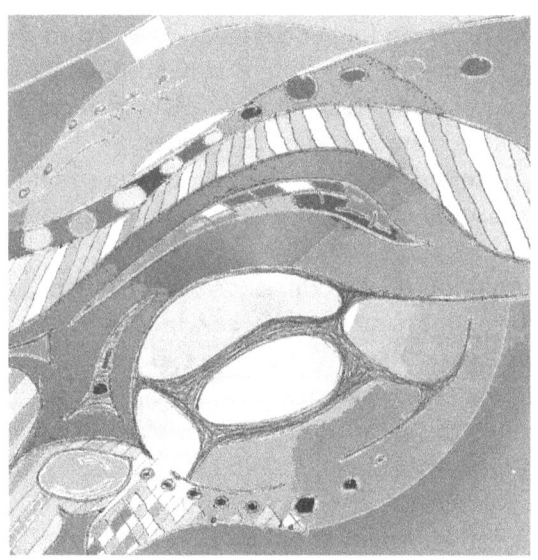

The Beautiful SIMPLICITY! (inc Identity, Essence, Joy, Vision)

There are more apparent paradoxes that can – as ever – be merged into one, and some I would like to mention here again.

- Simplicity / Complexity
- Surrender / Responsibility
- At-oneness / Freedom
- Torture / Bliss

Life can often seem very complicated, and hard to get a grip on. When we come across information that seriously questions our current views, it can even create cognitive dissonance as we struggle to process it and re-mould our overall picture to take it into account. However, if we regularly question things, and process our complex experiences and information sources, we can simplify things as we go.

In other places I write surreal poetry, where mind mixes ideas, objects, and situations and turns it all into some other sort of sense. This can often be a way to deal with difficult subjects such as political, or of trying to understand something that doesn't quite make sense in other ways, perhaps of odd memories.

I also write of psychic landscape where mind melds with nature and explores ambivalent feelings and plays with wild ideas.

I just wanted to register an awareness of these other sides of my expression of being-ness, because these show some ways of mentally and emotionally processing our experiences of life. Both of these approaches work brilliantly with children in writing workshops, and I believe it is very helpful to them to be encouraged to think and write like this, as it seems to appeal naturally to them. We are all unique in the ways we reach our own understandings of situations, and sometimes we may even decide it is okay to leave some things pending explanation. It may seem to make one's view of life more complex, but this is not the case, as we are processing things bit by bit instead of building up a torturous logjam that we can eventually make no sense of at all. Our brains feel that they are dealing with things so that they can surrender them and move on to the new. Everything boils down to a sense of having reached a personal balance of truth, through a freedom to express our experiences of this life. Your only responsibility is to be true to yourself, and your own vision of life here.   Once we have found the answers we are seeking, it all seems very simple after all, that is of course until next time we have to re-adjust to incorporate something new into the picture! Our personal & collective knowledge & experience never stops expanding, just like the universe.

 I have talked elsewhere of surrender vs responsibility, to show that surrendering is not a giving up of anything, it is in fact merely a shrinking of the ego's control over you to allow room for the real side of you to expand. This real side is connected to the loving energy of the source, so uses that love as its basis for life, thus you become much more responsible than ever as your intentions are purified. I wanted to remind us of this in this section, because, again, that reflects the simplicity and the blissful at-one-ness & freedom of being.

 I have been on work training on subjects such as attachment theory, where we have been asked to define ourselves, using circles within circles, and words in those circles to name things at the core of our identity, and things further out on the fringes that are still part of our identity. It struck me that mine was very different to most people's, but there was a strong similarity between mine and religious people, where they considered their religion to really be at the core of their being (and here I mean religious people who really were true to the finest human principles). I don't really like to use words to try to define what I am etc because it is too much like putting myself in a box – something I have by nature always resisted doing – but if I had to, I would describe myself as Spiritual or Mystical (in philosophy & practice). Most other people defined themselves according to what was around them or what had happened in their lives, such as being married, and having children. I considered those things as very important of course, but they were more like things I had chosen to do rather than things that made me who I am, so they had to be more peripheral in this process, whereas the fact that I feel safe in myself is right at the core of who I am. Not being tortured by fears allows me to step into bliss. First we are who we are, we then do things according to that. All our other relationships stem from our sense of self and how we interact with the world and others. Of course, we can sort of just let things happen to us, but if we think about it, we all make choices along the line to at least some degree, and we also tend to be curious.

 This is part of why I have been drawn to challenging jobs, travels, and many other things I might not try otherwise. I believe that life in the physical is given to us so that we can experience lots of things and grow from our experience, and I have an optimistic overall approach to life, in that I think it is for celebrating as well. I think we should notice all the wonderful things about us, and truly witness them in an honest & appreciative way, including the amazing mystery of life itself. So the other major thing I said was part of my identity is the fact that I feel connected to everything, including the earth, and a major part of who I am is the ability to experience & express creative joy.

Identity

I am part of the stream of consciousness. I overflow, I am everywhere, my atoms mixing with yours, and with nature and the elements – infinitely.

I am stardust, I am golden, and I walk right now in the beautiful garden.

I walk through lives and return and return to this earth to find new expressions of myself, new experiences to learn from, new ways of being invincible – for though I die it does not matter, I am only travelling again through the space of myself – contemplating the next path to take.

In this life, I am someone who sings and dances and paints, someone who goes to many places yet always feels safe. I am someone who feels at one with the natural world, who likes people but also likes solitude and space, who is fascinated by the seeming paradoxes of simplicity and complexity, at oneness and freedom, by our minds' twists and turns and games. I am one who is constantly amazed by the short gap between love and fear, torture and grace.

We are at one with creation, not bound up by anything. We are innocent and free to experience and express life in all its infinite variety. As we recognise the unity of all creation, so we see that there are no paradoxes – they are only illusions created by our minds until we surrender our petty dreams into the great peaceful one.

Life is a dance of self discovery. I am intoxicated by it. Love exists everywhere – I breathe it in, I breathe it out. Come dance with me in the universal sea of colour and movement – ecstatically free in each moment to be ourselves, yet embraced in a deep union. Miracles blaze in our eyes and hearts, for we are expressions of Love.

Realising all this, we no longer feel trapped in the world with all its weird and tragic goings-on's – we survive in it physically, but consciously we transcend it. We are no longer burning in the tortured chaos, but have transcended into the realm of bliss, where heaven is within us because we see everything as love, including ourselves.

Simplicity does not mean boredom. We don't seem to be able to reach absolute perfection on the physical plane, yet go on learning. As human beings we are in a sense perfectly human, as humans are inherently prone to making mistakes. Unless we do this, we can't learn, so in our new awareness we can allow life to go on teaching us how to go on showing up as our best, no matter what.

Someone who is steady and emotionally strong most of the time, still has blips into the other sides of these paradoxes – when something or several things at once happen to tip the balance, it's easy to momentarily forget what one has learnt. Or it could just be that time of the month – feeling tired and weak, or in pain – or just wanting to retreat from the 'world out there' for a bit.

But we have the tools and the skills to climb back up pretty quickly. And we have things that we can use as quick reminders to bring us back.

Try Meditating in the Heart. Try to empty it like one can do with the mind, then let everything flood in.

We are always seeking for some meaning or purpose in our lives. Poets go into the darkness and come out into the light – they see joy eventually – the meaning does not necessarily need to have purpose to allow us to feel joy. What we feel allows us to be what we are.

So – if you ever feel you have a desolate heart, just meditate on that emptiness – just let it be – and suddenly the dream of the whole universe fills it. You feel the joy of that totality. You don't feel sadness or pain, although those must be contained in there along with everything else, the joy overrides it completely, at least for the moment. You feel the incredible imperative of life flowing, in its most fundamental form, like an energetic grid, into everything.

Respecting Personal Identities

When we learn to love ourselves, not in a vain or narcissistic way, but simply in an accepting way, as a confirmation of who we are – we are acknowledging all parts of ourselves and saying "Okay, so this is me".

We accept all our different masks or personas (that we all exhibit in different situations) as these are all valid and useful parts of us.
Our egos are also valid and useful to us – they ground us for the practicalities of existence. They also provide a basis from which to expand our understanding of anything else.

Through our learning and our experiences, we build a reality around ourselves where we feel secure, but we also accept that this reality may evolve as we experience and learn more.

We respect ourselves for our balance and our choices, and allow others to make their own journeys as they see fit.

People we befriend tend to be those we respect and identify with (as having some sort of common reality), thus it is easier to get along with and spend time with them. But in the oneness of course, we *all* share a sense of common reality – we all stem from the same source. We embrace all that we are, and it embraces us.

Essence, Joy, Vision

Essence is the light of Spirit, and therefore all spirits (or souls). Every person, plant, animal, and even the earth itself – is interconnected, and anything that affects one part affects the whole.

Becoming aware of our essential nature means knowing our deepest identity. An increased state of consciousness allows us to find the essence of WHO WE ARE, and experience a more heavenly reality here & now.

Knowing the essential self means knowing the knower, being conscious of being conscious.

It also means appreciating what we witness and experience. Nisargadatta calls this "detached but affectionate awareness". It means paying attention in an accepting way, of everything you see, hear, smell, taste, feel, say, write, think, do. I love the word "affectionate" here. It helps us to keep "light", and love the world and each other despite everything that might otherwise seem crazy. It helps with detachment.

We should never judge those who are not yet aware of what they do. It is all down to intention really. It takes everyone time to become aware to this extent, and even then it takes a further age to try to only do what you would consciously wish to do, instead of reacting in the old way to situations.

The throat chakra (energy centre), seems to be in a blocked

state throughout most of our current civilization. If only we could communicate properly there would be less misunderstanding, argument, war. But at the heart of being able to communicate properly is the need for people to allow others to have their points of views, and to listen to them and take them into consideration instead of reacting against them. We usually react against things because they make us fearful, so if everybody was loving enough with each other to trust each person to simply be who they are, then they would not fear losing them, or worry about what they would think of them if they were also to simply be who they are. If we could all feel safe enough to speak our truth then communication would be so much simpler, we could say what we really meant, and expect understanding. If we realised that we are actually all in this together, it would not make any sense to try to compete against each other or control situations.

Mystics of all traditions claim that if we become conscious of our essential nature, we will see that actually there is only one of us. There is one self experiencing itself to be many selves! Zen masters say that there is one Big Mind within which the dream of life is arising. This includes everything, we should not reject any part of life in its wonderful variety. Everything has just as much right to exist as anything else, and it is all there for us to experience what we choose, and we should let others make whatever choices they wish.

Science and Spirituality are complementary and seem to be converging more in their conclusions. Sir James Jeans has said "The universe begins to look more like a great thought than like a great machine", and the great physicist Max Planck said decades ago that "There is no matter as such. All matter originates and exists only by virtue of a force which brings the particles of an atom to vibration. I must assume behind this force the existence of a conscious and intelligent mind. This mind is the matrix of all matter." And Schrodinger said that **we are spectators outside the material world and we only believe we are in it because our bodies are.** [His metaphorical cat is *potentially* both dead and alive, until the second we observe it. So we can believe whatever we will, and none of us need be in consensus, until we have reliable facts. Even the words 'dead' or 'alive' are seemingly paradoxical states, but in his cat experiment they either can exist simultaneously, or aren't actually real states, except perhaps in a very temporary fashion, applying only to a physical representation of something we have perhaps even dreamed.]

If we feel that we know our essence, then we can envision how everything we know might arise from one stream of consciousness, and being connected with that, we can witness with joy and fascination how so much variety brings beauty to our world. When you are connected to this stream, your awareness knows no fear or tug of opposites, it only feels that all is one in love. It is love in its purest sense because it is an overwhelming feeling of belonging and yet of having freedom to be as we choose, without judgement (just as in our most joyous relationships, uncontaminated by manipulations stemming from perceived needs and fears).

Perhaps we have come here just to learn about love – that everything is love – and that consciousness is enough – if everything is love then we are always home. Everything we need to do here can be better achieved through love.

When you are connected with the original stream, you can sense the bigger picture, the overall awesomeness. In the stillness, there are no boundaries, or limits, only joy.

If you are in a beautiful place suddenly you might feel a sense of connection with it all. For those of us who love the natural world, it can be a great soother. Some might respond to other beauty such as music, poetry, art... where some illumination from beyond shines through and connects emotionally with us.

It is perfectly possible to trigger visionary experiences and raise your state of consciousness at will. It is really quite simple to concentrate on one's breath for example, and give your mind time to still, then put out the intention for your mind to connect with the vast living consciousness within us all. Just breathe deeper and breathe it in, imagine it filling you and all around you. Look at the world with new eyes that see the life force throbbing beautifully everywhere. If you experience interfering thoughts, just set them aside gently and go on.

There is a huge variety of methods one can use to meditate and reach peak states. With practice you can eventually connect easily at any given moment, even while waiting in the post office queue for example. If you need to tackle something difficult, you can take those deep breaths of joy to centre yourself before you begin to act or speak. You can use visions for finding out all sorts of details as well, answers to deep questions for example, and all sorts of creative ways of enhancing your life!

Ideally deep breathing should feel as if it's going into the stomach, as your diaphragm goes down then comes up to release it.

 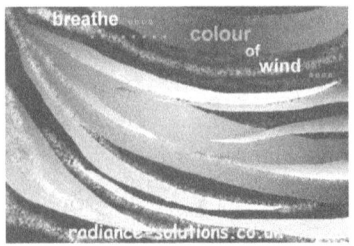

*Ideas are miraculous conceptions I cherish
like flowers in the desert sand that can grow or die
depending on whether we bring them water or not
and if we avoid trampling on them somehow.
But ideas can also be like fish that swim away in the light of morning.*

Here are a couple of artistic ideas for expressing identity:

This is a sort of personal mandala – the colour version includes colours
I feel in my aura, the most predominant usually being:
Yellow – denoting mental activity and/or self confidence,
Dark Blue – denoting intuition, and Purple – meaning spiritual.

*You can try creating your own by imagining the colours around you and in you -
it's sort of like stream of consciousness drawing / colouring.
If you don't think you can imagine colours, just pretend – you might surprise
yourself, but different things appeal to different people, so just try what you fancy.*

The colour version of this one has a lot of greens and yellows to represent my connection with nature and the sun, and the yellow in my aura (I'm a Leo – a fire sign). It also has ethnic type colours (like in beads & bits of leather) to show my link to South Africa, where I grew up, in the wonderful mountainous wilds.

This one is actually mostly blue and red in the colour version. I did it live at a storytelling week in the Harold Hillier Gardens.

The colour versions of my art can be seen on my websites & blogs.

You can live like a prayer
in thanks for life.
You can throw away fear
and trust yourself –
to be wide open –
like the whorls of a shell,
or a circle of petals,
or a starlit night.

You can exchange love with
the universe
in movement or in stillness.
You can renew your energy
and celebrate mind, spirit,
body – as one.
You can dance beyond your
boundaries,
breathing to release tensions
and invoke peace.

Breathe sunlight on lily pads
& water.
Dance the fiery ice of planets
spinning.
Feel like the divine child
singing,
or flow like the wise elder.

Dance like the rain and the
endless river.
Dance like the desert dunes
constantly re-shaping.
Breathe like the wind blowing
them,
or like the leaves of trees
across the world –

whose sap rises
with all the ingredients of life.

Let us dance to affirm our
wholeness,
to unite with our eternal
cosmos –
which is like a listening heart,
beating, circulating
consciousness.

Let us dance the changes
we make from moment to
moment,
the transformation, the
unfolding,
the becoming always new.

Let us dance the circle, the
centre,
the healing, the respect, the
blessing,
the laughter, the light, the
peace,
the experience, and the lesson,

the pure being, lifted –
expanding like the universe –
within, and all around,
connected, yet free,

living, glowing, breathing
magically,
flowering, opening our hearts
gracefully.

So, Why Are You Still Here? (Including Dropping Fear)

If you are alive then you still have something to learn from this lifetime or to do in it. This may mean nothing more than reflecting your personal perceptions of your experiences. This in turn further defines who you are being in relation to everything the stream of consciousness creates around you.

We can do this heavily, in a half-conscious state, or we can try to be more aware and choose now to sense the lightness and joy that seems to be present in the creative stream itself, and thus in everything natural. As children we feel this, but all too often our open innocence becomes polluted with tensions, pressures and material values.

If we become fearful, and struggle against, or attempt to resist things, or even try to block them by hiding behind addictions, then we create further difficulty for ourselves because this goes against the stream of life. However, if we can relax the ego and the clamour of the mind, then we can literally lighten up, and the stream of consciousness seems to work with us, reflecting our own joy back at us, and showing us its treasures.

Most of the pressures come from the expectations of others, but we can politely decline to accept these and find our own state of grace by living our lives in a way that we see fit, not listening to all those other voices, but trusting instead the whisperings of our own souls.

We should never judge others because they are only where they are at and doing what they are doing due to the sum total of their learning and experiences so far. The same applies to you, so anything that others might think is irrelevant.

If we are ONE with the Stream, God, or Universe, then we are everything and yet nothing. This is challenging for the logical mind to perceive, and frightening for the ego that wants to hold onto everything physical. Everything vanishes except consciousness…….

But it starts again. We come from nothingness and return to nothingness – yet the cycle is infinite. Poets strive to understand this, artists, scientists, anyone who is driven to try to gain some understanding of the universe, and / or our minds. If we can put the ego and our logic into the background a little, letting them do their jobs but not rule us, then we can allow our heart-centred awareness to open up into wider consciousness and bloom fully.

In this blossoming, we come to know things that help us to drop our fears, and embark on deeper journeys of exploration. We are then prepared to leave behind some of our clockwork worlds and make some real discoveries. We begin to truly celebrate the wonderfulness of our universe because of the amazing abundance and diversity, and we can literally play a hand in creating our own reality.

Perhaps there are multiple varieties of yourself in different dimensions living out the other versions of your life as if you had all made different choices, or perhaps accentuating different skills….. perhaps there is a musician, an artist, a scientist, a mathematician, a volunteer, a road sweeper, and a big business mogul out there. Perhaps you can call in advice from their experience into your life now?

Perhaps we can do whatever we want to with our minds? Perhaps we can change the nature of things, create whatever set of events we wish?

Perhaps you are still here to help claim back our world (Gaia) as a home for all species, including ourselves, to live in peaceful balance (symbiosis)? Surely conscious evolution should be about trying to find ways of doing this?

So, why are you still here?
Is there more to learn, or more to do, or both?

You are a super-conscious multidimensional being –
YOU decide.

I step into the night to witness the beauty of the stars. If I don't go into the darkness, how can I come back new? Within space is infinite unborn energy – this is what I sense inside my body.

Where is the stuff that was inside my mind? It is easily lost yet equally easy to find! There is nothing impossible in unbound time.

I am the nothing within the seed of all creation, yet no matter how deep I sleep, love always awakens me, eventually.

I am the contemplation and the perfection of my own destiny. I am the fusion of silence and activity. I am unity.

I breathe in cycles like the cosmos returning to the heart of the original sea of dreams – and springing forth again with abundant life.

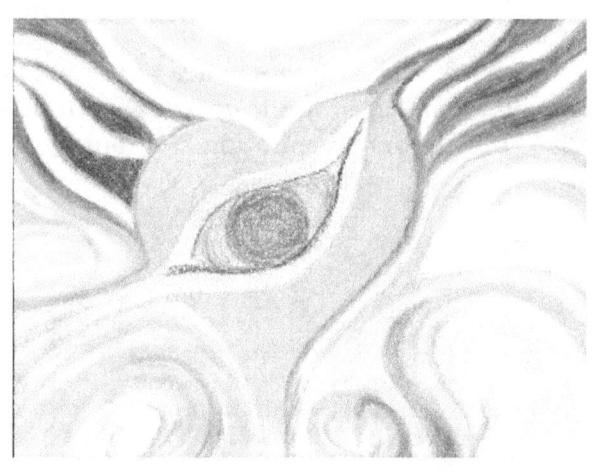

Healing the Tears IV

When you want the clock to stop stealing your life, try climbing a mountain.
When you want the walls of the fortress to crack, try singing or smiling.
When you want a path to lead you out of the mire, just start walking.
Anything you desire could be round the corner. If you don't look you might miss it,
so please pay attention every step of the way to what's going on around you,
there might be a vote you can take, or something you need to do,
to make some sort of difference.

Swallow the daylight into your body, for it may not come again tomorrow.
How do we know that the skylark will call once more in the distance?
How can we tell if a man will return from his travels, or never come back?
We know only that one thing leads to another and that minutes tick by,
but in the silence of each of those minutes, we can drink in mountains and seas,
we can grow flowers out of our heads, and feed kind composting words to our hearts,
we can mean more than we ever thought possible to believe.

So you need to be strong – peace to ground you and courage to act from the centre of your being.
I offer some inspiration and tools:

> Don't be afraid to be authentic,
> show up in the world as you truly are.
> Be as you mean to be, but be light with it.
> Love it, give it, share it, laugh at it,
> walk everywhere with it.
> Be in the world but not OF it.

> "Don't let anyone take your power by influencing what you do.... sure ask for advice when you are still deciding, but once you are sure what you want to go for, don't let anyone deflect you. It is YOUR choice to make and to follow through."

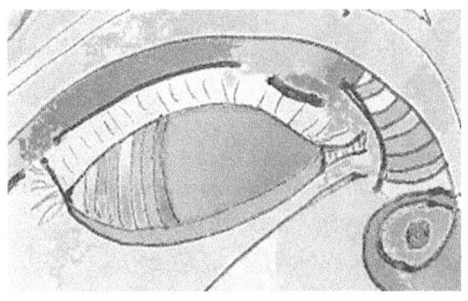

Look the world right in the eye!

**Our true nature
is one of innocence
and freedom to choose
how we live.**

We need to be brave enough
not to give that away.

**Don't give up
on your right to and sense of**
TRUTH, JUSTICE, and GRACE

Responsibility –
your ability to respond to life – can be enhanced in so many ways!

Don't be afraid.
You are never really alone.
Just be yourself.
You don't ever have to pretend
you're someone else.
If you try to do that then you
don't have anything
you can give the world.
Accept & Give your Gifts with Love.

I want to express the gifts I have been given to share here with anyone who wants them. Pay it forward. Circulate. Trust.	**Abundance & Nurturing** I draw more nurturing experiences towards myself. Using my best skills nurtures me as well as others.

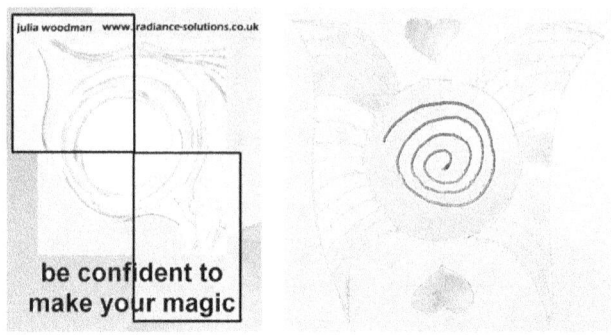

Be Heart Centred – Keep your Balance.
Be Graceful amidst the Chaos.
Don't let other people steal your energy –
Don't give your power away.
Remember that it's your choice what to do / how to respond.
Be yourself – Trust your own Truth.
Be grateful for, and enjoy, everything & everyone around you.

Your path may weave its way, but you can choose how to walk it.

> **Don't let fear of what others might think add to your negative self talk!**
>
> Shrug off criticism
>
> Oh well - I am me
> and you are you -
> **x x x**
>
> At the end of the day,
> **you don't have to please anybody but yourself** -
> we are our own best judges
> of how we want to be in this world.
>
> **Trust yourself and be in your own truth.**

*Try to be the best version of yourself
for your own sake, no one else's.
Don't expect perfection,
just be awake and open
so that you keep finding ways to evolve
your patterns of thinking and being,
so that you can truly love
and trust yourself in this world.
In each moment that you breathe
remember to be your own best self.
Believe you can be.*

> You have everything you need
> inside you already -
> you may just need a little help
> to find, organize, and follow it.

Do I always follow my own advice? Heck no, sometimes I get caught up & forget for a while, just like everyone else, but I keep trying, and keep learning. I'd love it if you'd join me on the continuing journey.
I'm listed on Goodreads as Jay Woodman
where you can see loads more of my quotes.
I also put short quotes of mine, and of others
on Twitter @WoodmanJulia
- plus links to loads of info on all my social media networks -
Pinterest, Facebook, Google, Tumbler, etc
- and I run these Blogs –
createhealth.news & radiancesolutions.com

ENHANCING OUR LIVES

**Here are some Visualizations & Affirmations
to help maintain a sense of love, peace, and balance.**

They can be made into packs of cards if you like, and chosen at random, or used deliberately. They can be fun to give to friends, or as a lucky dip for visitors, asking them to choose without looking, from a tin perhaps... especially the affirmations.

Visualizations are like mini guided meditations. They should be used to ground you through an appreciation of nature, or other lovely things, if you become stressed, or too caught up in the false realities we allow to perpetuate around us when our guard is down.

Sit quietly and use them as a basis for brief meditations – taking yourself off on little journeys to unwind your mind. Use all your senses, and imagine the natural colours, scents, and sounds – flowing into your body to renew you, and feel your connection with the earth through your feet. Imagine the tensions of your body draining away.

Affirmations should be chosen carefully to help you change your ideas about your reality in the way that you specifically want to. Try using some of ours or alter them a bit to suit you specifically. Use one or two each morning and evening until you believe what you are saying. You can of course, also make up your own, but they must always be in the present tense.

Using positive tools like meditation & affirmations can re-train our minds & bodies to relax & listen to the whisper of our souls and seek our unique answers.		"Dance your Soulful path and you shall know the magic of your mind & heart, and all the beauty laughing to fill your rising self."

VISUALIZATIONS

Please sit comfortably with both feet on the ground, shut your eyes, breathe slowly & deeply, but gently, letting your stomach rise then fall with your diaphragm, relaxing every part of your body in turn.

Forest
Imagine you are walking through a forest.
Sunlight is sifting through fragrant green leaves.
Birds are singing.
Find a comfortable warm spot to rest in.
Watch, listen, and enjoy.

Ocean
Imagine you are walking along a beach.
Salty smelling waves are rolling rhythmically towards you.
Their sound induces a deep sense of tranquillity.
Find a comfortable warm spot to rest in.
Simply watch, listen, and enjoy.

Moon
Imagine you are sitting in a moonlit garden.
Small beautiful night sounds fascinate you.
The moonlight paints everything silvery.
You feel incredibly peaceful.
Simply watch and enjoy.

Mountain
Imagine you are on top of a mountain.
A warm wind is blowing any clouds away from you.
You feel the wind on your face and in your hair.
Enjoy the details of the view.
You feel uplifted.

Garden
Imagine you are walking through a gorgeous garden.
The sun is shining.
The colours and scents are exquisite!
Find a comfortable spot to rest in, and enjoy it!

Field
Imagine you are entering a field.
The grass is long and luscious, but dry.
There is a friend waiting there for you,
(or your inner child, or your higher self, or an animal.)
Play together there in the sunshine.
You are filled with delight and a sense of freedom.

Stream
Imagine you are walking beside a splashing stream.
You can see fish and dragonflies and birds.
The sounds wash away any tensions from your body.
Keep walking or stop for a rest, it's up to you.
Watch, listen, and enjoy.

Cloud
Imagine you are lying on top of a white cloud.
It is fluffy and cool and amazingly comfortable.
It is also incredibly quiet.
You forget all the troubles of the world.
You feel a deep sense of serenity.

Boat / Lake
Imagine you are drifting on a lake in a rowing boat.
You are comfortable and relaxed.
The gentle lapping sound of the water on the bottom of the boat
is like a lullaby to your ears.
Simply listen and enjoy.

Rainbow
Imagine you are flying through a blue sky.
The air is fresh after a rainstorm and birds are singing.
You approach a rainbow and sit on the very top of its arch.
Use all of your senses to enjoy the colours.

Waterfall
Imagine you are standing close to a waterfall.
You can feel the spray on your hands and face.
It is fresh and rejuvenating.
You feel so grateful and glad to be alive.

Desert
Imagine you are amongst magnificent orange sand dunes.
The sense of space and peace is incredible.
Find a comfortable hollow to rest in.
Simply watch, listen, and enjoy.

Snow
Imagine you are looking out upon crisp fresh snow.
Everything seems new and clean.
You realize that each new day does bring a fresh new chance.
We can do anything we really want to with our lives.
You smile with relief and gladness.

Sunrise
Imagine you are up early watching the sun rise.
The air is crisp and clear and you feel deeply refreshed.
You are sitting on a garden bench.
You have a blanket snuggled around you so you are not cold.
The colours are exquisite.
You feel very special and privileged.

Candle
Imagine you are gazing into the flame of a candle.
It seems as if the heart or soul of a friend is caressing you.
You may remember some special glad times.
You feel warm and safe, with love surrounding you.

Special
Imagine you are in a magic painting.
You are fit and gorgeous with great skin and flowing hair!
You are surrounded by beautiful flowers.
You feel incredible joy, love, and contentment.

Friends
Imagine you are sitting with close friends.
Choose your own setting (Park/Lounge/Restaurant).
Feel their love and laughter surrounding you.
You smile. You feel warm and safe.

Space
Imagine you are out in space.
You do not need anything – you simply float.
You are surrounded by beautiful stars and planets.
You feel incredible awe and love.

....be as free as a butterfly....

AFFIRMATIONS

Choose a few at a time to help you re-programme your thinking
and work towards goals – say them to yourself, and believe!
Affirmations always need to be in the present tense.
You can write them on little cards to keep with you, or put in special
places, even give to friends. Write your own specific ones too!

I release all past fears and resentments.
I open myself as a channel to the light.
I am free to create love in all that I do.
I trust in the power and magic of the universe.
I am open to receive.
Life is a miraculous gift!
I am listening to the whispers.
I am grateful, expectant, and intuitive.
I love. I trust. I have the best intent.
I walk with grace, and lightness of being.
I am a spark of the oneness.
If I need answers, I ask, and the light comes to me.
I am here to learn, grow, and have fun.
I am responsible for creating my own happiness.
I deserve to take good care of myself.

I nurture my body and feed my soul.
I make the time to be still, and listen to the truth.
I am one of many, but the many are also the one.
I take control of my own life.
I am confident, but humble.
*I do not swallow anger or hold resentment -
but deal with it constructively.*
Talking it out – heals.
I express myself clearly and positively.
I forgive others and myself, and let pain go.
I am dignified and compassionate.
I am walking in the light of love, joy, and laughter.
I am whole.
I speak from the heart.
I give from a sense of abundance.
I am realizing my dreams.
I live in a loving universe.
I trust the spirit of life.
I replace fear and guilt with courage and faith.
I love myself for being the best I can be.
I accept the power of the present moment.
I have plenty of time.
I am loving, powerful, and creative.
I dare to be myself – the truth of my own being
is stronger than anything.
I am becoming more and more of who I can be.
I am becoming more and more playful and happy.
I do not submit my integrity to anyone or anything.
I'm attracting more & more love, joy, humour, and abundance
into my life.
I love the world around me.
I delight in my success and the success of others.
I love. I am loved. I am free.
I accept criticism without letting it hurt or offend me.
I look at criticism objectively & accept only that part of it which is true.
We are all human – I do not expect myself to be perfect!
*I am enough. What I do is enough. Who I am is enough,
and yet I am always open to learning more & evolving.*
I trust my worthiness.
I appreciate the opportunity to learn and grow.

I respect and appreciate those around me.
I love being with my friends and family.
I praise the positive and give compliments where due.
I am nurturing, balanced, and decisive.
I am relaxed, loving, and intuitive.
I am learning to love myself without judgement.
I have decided to be happy despite everything.
I relax and appreciate.
I don't need addictions to fill gaps.
I feed my strengths and starve my weaknesses.
I release all grief to the Divine.
I am ready to move forwards.
I trust the universe to show me the next step.
I am willing to be responsible for what I accept into my life.
I open myself to new energy, people, places, experiences.
I am not afraid to change my life!
I can do anything I dream of doing.
My life has a purpose and I am here to fulfil it.
I deserve to give myself credit.
I live in the light of my truth.
I take joy in my success, and learn from my difficulties.
I make space to appreciate my life, and to be grateful.
I wish all my friends and family Delight & Magnificence.
The essence of my spirit is light and peace.
I seek the highest truth and the most healing ways to live.
The universe is in me, above me, and all around me, always.
I listen to my inner voice and visions.
I create clarity of mind and unlimited vision for myself.
Communication is vital to my wellbeing.
I pay attention to what is really precious.
I let my words come from my heart and stay with truth.
It's okay to be me. I know what is best for my body, mind, soul, and if I need new information or ways to change, I seek it out.
I am safe in the world.
I trust myself to make the best of things.
I ride the waves of life with grace.
In the core of myself there is freedom, peace, and love.
My spirit is eternal. It lives in grace and harmony.
I do not fear wild thoughts, as they can give rise to wondrous contemplation, creative endeavour, life changing ideas, momentous bliss.

I notice beauty everywhere everyday.
I breathe deeply and am grateful for each moment.
I am awestruck by our amazing world, how our bodies work, how there is everything we need available in the natural world.

What we focus on prevails, so I focus on my dreams and not small fears, which I can easily overcome anyway.
All shades are part of the one, it is only our views that try to make small separate realities, so I expand beyond artificial limits.
I am fine tuning myself to reach my peak frequency, and sustain balance of heart, mind, body, spirit.
I constantly balance myself to be at max potential in any situation.
The light in me recognises the light in others.
I do not take offence over small cheese, I let things slide off when they don't really matter, don't take things personally, remain untainted, free.
I pause to ensure my response is not reactive.
I don't need to defend anything, I relax my story and dissolve barriers.
My soul is infinite, so cannot be threatened.
I can always choose differently.
If someone seems to want to hurt me, I ask myself what could be hurting them so much.
I make the best of things. I learn, I cope, I am fine.
My heart & soul are linked to my mind to enable it to do what is best for me in all ways, beyond just bodily & mental function.
I define what my own reality is.
Life is an adventure I am enjoying creating.
I allow humour to dance lightly in my heart.
I regularly clarify with myself what is important to me so that I can keep on track, and be grateful for the positives.

Relaxing your membranes (or meme brains – mind attachment to stories you might have been telling yourself).

We have layers of energy, surrounding our bodies, to create auras. They become denser as they get closer to our physical bodies. We need to remain open, not shut off, through fear etc hardening or tightening these layers. We need to just use them as filters, allowing an interaction with the world around us, in much the same way as osmosis works within all our cells. If we are afraid or uptight, trying to control and protect, we tend to put up extra mental barriers, or block those filters, mistakenly separating ourselves from the rest of the universe. If we disconnect in this way from our vast, supportive source, then we shrink or limit our potential, and may also become unwell. We need to keep connected to our greater selves or deeper consciousness, where everything is interconnected and whole, beyond any issues our smaller selves may have. Fear can come in many shapes & forms – such as fear of losing something or someone (an object, a person or relationship, a job, status or position, money or other benefits, means of security such as your home etc, control of a situation, our youth, our health, our own bodies, or fear of losing hold of who we are trying to project ourselves to be). Of course there are other logical fears (not really relevant here) that come to warn us of actual danger such as crocodiles, so that we can take steps to avoid them or deal with them, and these should not be ignored, but nor should they be overblown.

So, if our ego reacts to what other people may think about us (whether real or imagined), or to criticism (taking offence instead of looking to see if we can learn anything valid from it before letting it go), then we are putting up these barriers, and causing ourselves to seem more separate than we actually should be. But what are we really defending? What is this ego really, with its imagined need to hold onto things or situations? Who are these people around us, but simply other forms of energy, just like ourselves, with their own fears, doubts, and loves. We are all vulnerable, so if we can recognise & accept that, we should be able to avoid creating dramas. So breathe, breathe, let those membranes relax. Accept that you are part of the infinite universe and rejoice in that. Let the barriers and the masks fall away. Feel free to be who you want to be without any stressful need to try to manipulate or control things around you, just let it happen. Walk in the light of who you are in spite of everything, regardless of what happens, or what others do, or may seem to think. If we can relax those barriers, maybe even dissolve them, we will then find we are more at peace with the world. We can also redirect the energy it was draining from us (to maintain them) into more positive things, and open up to more love, trust, friendship, and personal appreciation of life, beauty, and the incredible stuff all around us. Relax and give thanks for the opportunity to interact with all of it. Breathe, breathe, and relax those membranes. Let the infinite universe flow around and within you, as it is meant to, renewing your life force, and allowing it in turn to flow back with its information about who you are being, what you are experiencing, how you are feeling. Would you want that information to be a scrambled mess of tense emotions? Surely not. So let it be a clear message of how at peace you can be with life, how you can live it as an open human being, learning, appreciating, growing, loving.

Gangaji says "If our story makes us feel wronged or victimized, then we suffer. If your life is about protection from pain, then your life is about suffering. But you have the conscious choice to release yourself from the trap of suffering & anger. Tell yourself the truth of who you are. There is no need to be a victim. Meet your experiences without hiding or running or wailing or justifying or cursing, just meet them. Recognise that all is composed of thought – it's a story. Are you willing to just call it off?"

Mooji says "Consciousness is not a slave to the mind's projections, stories, imagined requirements. Consciousness relaxes, doesn't have to make decisions, it follows spontaneous urges and is carried forwards. Consciousness … is beyond…. Constant…. Unattached…."

You cannot interrupt the flow of the universe. If you put up resistance you only cause more problems, issues, blocks. So, create within the natural flow, make the best of the current available.

Mooji says "The world is awake….. even in your own heart…. There is always something that is beyond…. All change ….. you observe, you witness, you are aware…. Of things passing…. Even knowledge, even personality, emotions, beliefs; something that is beyond healing, birth, death, that is undying, unbroken…." Plus he advises "Marinade yourself in the presence, beyond everything, no fear, no need, pure awareness." And "You are in direct oneness with yourself…. Your uniqueness does not interfere with the oneness of being. It sings its magnificence – that even on one flower each petal is unique. We are expressed uniquely in form but have one common source…."

So, if we can relax & let ourselves be part of the flow of consciousness, we can recognise, feel, that all of us belong to that same flow, and see beyond the little 'I' personalities to a deeper shared ground. We can let go of all that we had thought was wounded, and any imagined need to try to control things.

Gangaji says "Stop that story about your emotions, it's all a narrative… you stop that and then there's a possibility to find real clarity. Just stop that, and experience what you're feeling." She also says that collective justice is the deeper question, the real issue in our world, not the tiny personal problems, whether we get our way or not. She suggests we "shift our allegiance to the eternal presence of our being", and says "Your soul longs to know again what was once purely and absolutely known to be the truth of who one is," and "Each story will end, but you are the clear light that story appears in."

Mooji says "There is no judgement, all things come and go, including feelings."

Gandhi said "There is a force in the universe which, if we permit it, will flow through us and produce miraculous results."

Now you are good and strong and steady -
ready to look the world right in the eye.
Ready to do whatever you think you need to do
to keep what you love alive.

A brief look at Handling Change

These times are moving fast and many things are changing around us. Also, as beings who wish to become completely true to ourselves, there are going to be changes we want to make anyway. Your heightened awareness will make you see things much more clearly, and it will also give you more confidence and a sense of personal power. If you discover new information about the world, you may decide to take a stance – to live differently. You may wish to become active in helping to make changes where you think that change is needed in society, or you may wish to become more self-sufficient and to step out of systems that others have imposed on us. Or you might wish to make other changes, for example in your personal life or in your work/life balance. Change is completely natural; please don't be afraid to enter the adventure.

Aside from this section in this book, my book, **"Back to The Garden"** will continue from here, and www.backtothegarden.org.uk and an open facebook group have been set up, where you can join in with sharing knowledge and information about what is going on in our world and ideas about how we can do things differently.

We encourage global meditation link ups by setting times where people can join in from wherever they are to focus on planting positive thoughts into the collective consciousness (subtle activism). We have links to many other websites providing useful information, particularly ones which provide ideas and information to help with positive change.

My other books will also contain many further ideas relating to personal & spiritual development or growth, and holistic wellbeing.

The Dancing Gardener

SAPLING (June 2011)

Drawn up out of the ground
By my consciousness,
Held by universal light,
Gently balanced –

Like a shoot growing,
Opening to life,
To the possibilities
Of blossoming and seeding.

My life-stream flows
From past to present
Informing me of choices
Made and lived –

And more to take now;
Crossroads to be stood at
Gazing in different directions
Before progressing;

Wondering how much difference
It actually makes
As long as I am the one
In the driver's seat

Being complete in who I am,
For I have chosen
To be here, living
Like a sapling drawn to the light.

Imagine your Magic Tree!

Will it feed you, will it give you energy?
Will it hold all sorts of secrets
In its leaves, its sprouting canopy?
Will it have hidden messages
wrapped up in its seeds?

And what about the flower's power?
What is that to be?

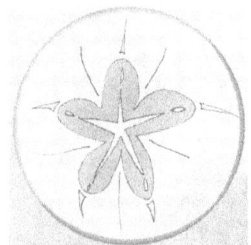 

CONSCIOUS EVOLUTION

ONE – (Self in the World)
This is where everything starts, with you, one of many.

It's easy to love your friends, and for them to love you, but what about you loving you? Are you good at that? You need to be, because YOU MATTER.

Hopefully this would not be some egotistical you who stroppily wants everything to go your way and doesn't care much about how that affects others, and not a you who bows down to please everyone for fear of losing friends either – but a balanced you who would like to manage to fit into this world without having to hugely compromise your own ideas and standards, but who is open enough to be willing to learn and evolve.

Hopefully this would also be a you who is learning to listen to your inner voice trying to guide you. (Ignoring what it wants to tell you, or suppressing any pain or anguish it may be trying to express, can only ever be a temporary coping mechanism, eventually leading to worse pain, conflict, or other consequences.). Treat it as a partner (accept it and face up to the truth of whatever it has to say), and it will lead you into healing clarity, and help you to find your true self with a great sense of confidence in where you are going / who you are being.

Who you are being in this world matters a great deal – not to others, but to YOU. It can help to take stock now & then of what your main ideals, principles, and aims are, as these can change along the way. You can then assess if the person you see in the mirror is on the track you have chosen, or if some adjustments need making. You don't need to be perfect, but going in the general direction sure helps!

Meditation to love one's self:

- You are in a good mood, light hearted, full of spirit.
- You are out for the evening at a good music (or other) event, looking forward to some dancing or good company and chat (or whatever makes for a good evening for you).
- You see friends across the room and go over to greet them.
- You are particularly warm, walking with bounce, smiling and reaching out as you approach.

- You take their hands, hug them, whatever is appropriate for each.
- You chat with some of them for a while.
- You then see yourself entering the room from the other end.
- You hesitate, but only for one second!
- You go over and greet yourself in the same way you just did with your friends.
- All of you stand or sit together, talking, and watching as the band sets up, or whatever your chosen event is unfolds.
- It is a great evening of good companionship, bonhomie, and fun.
- You say farewells fondly all round before going home and having a good night's sleep.
- In the morning you feel refreshed (write down anything else you may feel or any insights you may have).
- Do you decide to do anything as a result of this?

Can you see how easy it is to love yourself without letting all sorts of things get in the way if you just do it? We don't expect our friends to be perfect do we – we love them just as they are. None of the details matter in the moment – you just greet them and have fun together. You quite naturally make allowances in the joyful flow of events.

And the world:

We can be in love with the world like this. It is bitter sweet – but it is just as it is for this moment. We love that moment too – there is no reason right now to think of anything more than loving things just as they are.

Another day you might like to look more into the world and notice all the amazing detail in things, how your body works, how the natural world all fits together, the wonders of growth, colours, textures, scents, sounds, and tastes.

Let your curiosity run wild – explore!

- Life is a mystery just as it is!
- Feel how amazing that is – feel how peaceful it is just to accept it.
- Feel the contentment unfolding.

Communication with the higher level:

You can always communicate with a higher (or deeper) level of yourself if you are feeling stuck. There are many ways of doing this. Here are a couple.

1) Simply sit quietly, breathe deeply to relax and then imagine you are having a conversation with yourself. Ask yourself for advice on any situation.
1a) One way of doing this is to actually move from one chair (or cushion) to the other as if you are play acting to be talking to yourself in the other chair.
1b) Another way is to have the intention (ask the universe to allow this to happen) of speaking with your wise higher self. You might like to imagine a setting you would enjoy, like by a log fire in a pub, or out in a grassy field. You don't have to speak out loud, just do it in your head.

2) Another thing to try is to imagine you are communicating with some other wise person, and asking them for advice. Note that the wise person is simply another version of yourself who is easier for you to accept or imagine – the person would most likely resemble some symbolic figure to you, for example Merlin, or a Goddess. It is probably easier to imagine this if you first imagine walking into some place to meet them, like a wood, a castle, or a mountain top. It quite often happens that the wise person may give you advice as well as a gift that means something to you in a symbolic way. (See "Meeting the Helper" poem a bit later on.)

* NOTE – you can also imagine having a conversation like this with the higher self of another person, for example if you want to resolve an issue between you, or ask for forgiveness, or forgive them. Next time you meet you will find that the issue has magically vanished!

We can each have our own personal relationship with the universe, or the divine (whatever name you may give it).

We can always ask for insight from the universe around us. You might like to think of it as God or you might like to think of it as the Source of all knowledge, but whatever way you look at it, it is the same thing really. Just ask for help as if you were praying, but don't be selfish with it – always give love as much as you receive. Simply say "I love, and I am loved", then FEEL it. Just feel the connection open up between yourself and the universe – you might feel it mostly through your heart, or the top of your head, or just the sense of warm arms around you, or you might feel it coming in with every deep breath. It makes you forget the little stuff when you share this huge love. It lifts you up and makes it easier to cope. It makes you grateful too. It puts things in a wonderful perspective – there is this HUGE universe, and there is little you – but the love between you is just as important both ways. When you are truly balanced you can say "I AM love".

Life is Sacred – discover your innate uniqueness alongside a sense of deep belonging.
The ego just needs to relax a little, realise it doesn't have to fear the spiritual, as it makes you strong, whole.
If you know who you are then your ego feels safe instead of fearful, and is more open to exploration.
Affirmations:
My ego is a servant, not a ruler.
I accept my true purpose in life and aim to find all the best ways to fulfil it – study, tools, being open, curious, doing it.

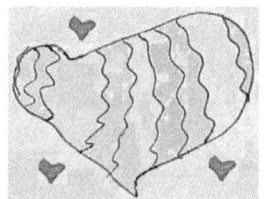  

There are many other tools we can use to help us keep steady & evolve. I have a sacred perspectives guide available, plus several other guides.

Reminders that Bring us Back

Someone who is steady and emotionally strong most of the time, still has blips into the other sides of these paradoxes – when something or several things happen at once to tip the balance, it is easy to forget what one has learned. Or it could just be that time of the month – feeling tired and weak – and all one wants is to retreat from the 'world out there' for a bit. **But we have the tools and the skills to climb back up pretty quickly. And we have things that we can set to use as quick reminders to bring us back.**

Movement / Breath

There is a form of movement called Mentastics (derived from the two words, mental gymnastics) which aims to train people with physical restrictions to move differently by training the mind in conjunction with the body. Anyone can use this method to tune in and move intuitively and develop wonderful dances or flowing exercises.

There is a key phrase that can be used to shift yourself into this intuitive state, whether playing squash, struggling with paperwork, or giving a talk… it is to ask yourself: "What can be lighter than this, what can be free-er than this?" This allows body and mind to move into soft time, where everything seems to just flow naturally and effortlessly, and the struggle is gone. Just keep on asking yourself until you feel you are in what athletes call **'the zone'**, or plugged into the vital creative cosmic source. You can use some of your flow time to get things done, or learn with ease and clarity; and some to relax, play, nourish, integrate, appreciate, and receive new inspirations. All of it should be joyful and fulfilling. We are fully alive, part of the ALL that IS, present in the Presence, translucent with the splendour of the ONE.

Movements can be chosen to incorporate feelings of grace and a flow of energy between body and mind. Just moving intuitively can do this, dancing freely to music, or moving in silence – you can copy nature, such as wind in the trees, or plants growing, or water flowing over stones, or fishes swimming, or animals bounding.

Movement work stemming from the martial arts traditions such as tai chi are good for this too, as the focus is on your centre of balance being just below your belly button, so that you crouch low and then move outwards from this. They call the flow of energy in the body the CHI, or breath, or life force, which is the same as what we are teaching to be everywhere around us as well as within us. The movements then incorporate the drawing in of energy from the universe, the movement of it all around the body, the giving out of our own pure heart energy to others, then returning to the central state of balance.

Breathing is a very important part of this. Good breathing enhances the movements. It also cleanses the body and adds to your general balance. The same applies to yoga.

The body is your temple for life. You have the divine right to wellness, wholeness, and soundness of body, mind, and spirit. You can imagine if you like, that you were created from a perfect template or blueprint that still exists energetically as your guiding principle. This is how your cells – which started out as being all the same – knew how to grow, or morph, into the right cells for each part of your body.

Apart from exercise, eating a balanced diet is a gift to yourself, to enhance the wellness of your body, the seat of your existence.

The universe turns out to be a timeless and infinite place where things are created again and again – look at nature and the cycles of the seasons – isn't it obvious really? There is birth and rebirth everywhere, even of stars! New ones are continually being formed. Dance with the universe to set your soul free.

Lighter

Dance and feel your limbs.
Think "what can be lighter
than this?"
and dance again,
thinking "what can be free-er?"
and dance some more –
letting your mind help you move
with grace across the floor,
light and free as a feather,
easily, don't try too hard,
it's easy to be
dancing like the spirit
that lifts you from within,
rhythmic and effortless,
expressive and balanced,

Now float and bounce,
let go of tensions,
open instead to fully living,
shimmering with body-mind
expansiveness.

Play, explore, discover,
feel your tissues respond,
feel the change as you dance.
There is nothing, there is
everything,
there is a fountain, there
is a spring,

There is an intimacy
which sets your being completely
free.

Swing with the motion, bend,
open, feel the rotation,
follow with eyes, glowing
eyes of inspiration.

You are aware and lovely,
in gentle momentum
like rocking a baby to sleep,
deep, beautiful sleep.

"What is softer?"
what is a more beautiful way
of knowing, feeling, moving,
projecting joy and ease,
allowing your body to be
dancing in a meditative flow,
a stream of peace,
at one with the dynamic energy
force
which surrounds and enters us all.

Wind, unwind, take your time,
give of your time, expand,
show your hands, simply,
effortlessly, giving, receiving
love and energy
in natural cycles.

Tai Chi and martial arts are great for conscious use of energies in movement.

Our CROWN and other areas

Anytime, when standing in a queue even, you can just reconnect to the source by imagining a light beaming onto your head (crown) or shoulders or back of neck, with all that loving energy in it that you want to remember is always there in your heart.

Or you can imagine it beaming into your solar plexus and sacral chakra areas (just above & below the belly button) if lying in the sun on the beach.

Or if sitting in a garden feel it pouring into your heart from the greenery and flowers around you.

Or if out for a walk, absorb it from the mother earth through your feet and draw it upwards into your body, via your root chakra (at the base of your spine).

What chakras are now left out? Oh the throat one – well now – here is a fantastic opportunity to use this one. When having a conversation, imagine the light shining there, the clear light blue, like fabulously clear water, rinsing through everything you want to say, so that it comes out crystal clear.

We can use the deep blue brow chakra in conversation too – shine it on other people when they are speaking so that you help encourage them to speak their truth with clarity. It also enables you to listen well to what they are saying. Give them the space to speak in their own time. Try never to get impatient and interrupt or say things for another person, as that is very disempowering for them.

It is good to imagine a protective bubble around you and state the intention that only good energy can come in; and that you cannot lose your own pool of energy, as it is always being replenished from the earth and the universe. The membrane of the bubble is permeable to allow the osmosis of good energy in both directions.

Meditation – There is a detailed guide available via our website – radiance-solutions.co.uk and I have created meditations for clients, which are posted on YouTube & SoundCloud.

Meditation is not a tool to control your minds, or suppress thoughts, it is a tool to transform your whole inner and outer ability to cope with life. It opens you to being able to engage with the flow of oneness – eternal consciousness – effectively, instead of cutting yourself off from it!

Meditation is the best tool I can recommend to anyone to help find balance in their lives and to enable them to live in both the oneness and the separateness. You can feel the space of the universe within you rising with gentle power.

Remember to think positively as much as you can, even if you just start with a few moments each morning, and focus on being **grateful** for what you do have.

Rituals – some people benefit from these

- Use of Oils / other scents / stones or crystals / plants / candles.
- Wearing certain colours to reflect moods or energies needed.
- Certain times of day to be still and make time for these things.
- Grace moment at start of day to remind us to be thankful for our lives, and dear ones
- Healing – allowing yourself time to receive, as well as give.
- Special meals to celebrate / Time away to special places (don't have to cost a lot).
- Walks in nature, swims, whatever suits you – to reconnect with mother earth.
- Music / slow, soft time / time with special friends who understand your journey.

Use Keywords or phrases that bring back whole slices of meaning
Keep these handy somewhere. (In my stress busting guide I also discuss NLP.)

- Confidence / Compassion – Love of self and others.
- Acceptance / **GRACE** / Gratefulness.
- **Peace** of mind – **Forgiveness** of self and others.
- **Knowledge** of the complete Source / **Wisdom** to live by that.
- Authentic Power / Bliss / **Loving** / Essence.
- **RADIANCE** / Being / Awareness.
- Life design / **Living on Purpose** / Intention.
- Witnessing / **Trusting** your Visions.

Using the help of GUIDES, (and Ascended Masters)
There are many levels of potential guides available to us.

Some are personal: 1) A higher level of your soul-self that you aren't normally consciously listening to, but can become aware of if you become ready for guidance, or: 2) An aspect of someone who cares about you (from any time-frame). These can be people who have known you or have some common heritage or other bond with you, they may just be beings who are interested in your development. I use the word 'aspect' to denote that their whole being is not present, just a part of them. It's as if you were having a thought of someone else, but at the same time carrying on with your normal life – they can do the same, or in fact answer your call, and thus you are linked-in enough to interact (in heightened states of consciousness). You may even see an energetic imprint of them, as well as hear them, and feel their presence. This is usually an internal sense, rather than as if they were sitting opposite you. Think in terms of multi-layered consciousness, multi-dimensions, non-linear time – yet it happens easily.

Some are non-personal – from the highest levels of our collective consciousness. They are either: 1) Representatives of races from human history bringing you their teachings – such as American Indian, Aboriginal, Celtic, Mayan, Greek, Egyptian, and other ancient civilisations, or: 2) Beings from our dreamed reality. These can include anything from 'masters' to fairy, to animal, plant, or even element. You can access these at will, but if you need catalysts you could use cards or texts that are available to help. You will tend to find prompts in a synergistic way, so that you follow the links you need most at that time. You might find that you build a link with one or more at certain stages of your learning, and then change to call on others as you develop.

Links to guides can happen spontaneously, or you can make a link by asking for it – making the conscious choice to welcome help. Try not to be afraid if it happens spontaneously at first, trust in your own groundedness, breathe deeply, and pay attention with your whole being – not just your head, but your heart too. You can ask who they are and what they are there for, and anything else that may help reassure you. If anything does not feel right, just ask for the link to go. (If you ask a friend for help it is better than if she butts in unasked. If you are open to listening, then you are ready to find the advice useful, if you are not open to it then you may reject it.)

Guides are links in whatever way works for you to accept the wider being-ness, and knowledge available to you, whether it be deeper self-knowledge, or wider knowledge of earth, life, and universe.

Meeting the Helper

An old man walks beside me on the path
he walks at my left shoulder
his face is powerful
he wears a grey beard and a black cloak
we don't speak
I know why he is here
he hands me a mask carved from pale wood
it is a bull with huge curved horns
I will wear it when I go into the shadows
I need not be afraid
the horns will penetrate the jungle for me
I need the darkness to make the light whole
to make the person whole
to make the journey complete
and the bull needs my pure white milk
as the old man turns to go
I see a child in rags on the back of his cloak
arms reaching up behind her to hold onto him
bare toes pointing
that child is me

From my book TREES

We can maintain a **timeless connection with the natural world** which can help strengthen us and make us feel at home here.
     It helps nurture our spiritual connection with our planet, which can be very multi-sensory and indeed sensual.
     It also stimulates creativity of all forms, enabling us to express our response to the incredible variousness of creation, and explore our ambivalent relationships to it.
     And it helps us develop a meaningful psychological & philosophical understanding of all layers of ourselves, and our relationship with all things here.

In a Bishopswood Clearing

I am sitting in the grass with a picnic
basket and a notebook.
The children walk away from me
Flick-flickety off at a tangent
between thin blotched beech trunks,
then turn like yo-yos at the end of their strings
and come back to me.

Slabs of sun and shade slash
their faces as they come
but do not cut as deep as the flex
of their emotions
grappling with some
small understanding of this
place, this time, we're in.

From my book FOLLOWING FATHER

Waves at Hawkwood

This grass is like the sea.
I ride over it with big strides
uphill away from the spray of civilisation.
Deep breaths of green
rinse over my head and chest.

At the forest edge the water level rises;
trunks are awash with ivy.
The green sound of crows
flaps up from the valley
like wet raincoats.

Stalks bob buoyant heads
in the wind, and I take
the seed of their image
back with me towards the buildings,

where roses cling to life-raft walls.

I walk in the translucent water
of silence.
The wooded hill behind the house
a tall green wave
towering over the place.

From my book "IN TOUCH WITH WATER"

(note that the three lines in italics can also be a haiku)

A Morning in Spain

I think I have swallowed
half the moon
and a couple of stars.
Cockerels are crowing but it is still dark.
Cockerels see the dawn coming
long before we do.
They recognize the colours of sunrise
painted into their tails as mementos.
They greet their old friend, the sun,
with cries of delight
which I heartily approve of
even if I do have to get up to make coffee.
The shutters of the house are open wide
to let in the first light,
just as my heart is open to the world,
and the Spanish guitar will shortly
talk to me as I sit with it on the porch
in the half dark
gradually unveiling shapes
of cats and trees and rocks, as it pales
then becomes bright day.

From my book "SPANISH POEMS"

GATEWAYS

Envision your gateway anytime you need it. It symbolises new realms.
    Have a vivid picture in your mind – actually draw it if you can – or make a collage.

Bridge of Light
Beyond the gateway is a new place you can make into anything you want.

Through the Gateway

Relaxing, I breathe in white light. It takes some time, but eventually I am surrounded by a silver mist… I hear the dripping of water from the leaves of trees, I feel cool and refreshed.

I open my eyes to see a forest. Ancient trees, but not too close together, bare earth between them. Vines and hanging wisps like monkey ropes, and lichen, moss, emerald green leaves – but cool darkness as sheltered from the sun.

I get up and turn around and around just drinking it in. There are parrots calling out around me too. An ascended master – Merlin – steps forward and greets me – holding out both hands and taking mine. He leads me forwards to a pool beneath a canopy. The water is turquoise, and there is white at the edges like marble or scooped shell – mother of pearl. I step in, and swim downwards, leaving behind any residue of my past. I swim forwards deep underwater – while swimming underwater I can also see myself from a distance – from behind and below – a dark shape kicking through turquoise – a peaceful, refreshing turquoise – quiet under here so deep down – then I rise up at the far end of the pool, and step out.

There is a huge beautiful flower opening slowly to my left, and it continues to open as I gaze at it. Merlin is next to me again – with me – and he says that I am ready for my light body (to awaken) – so he puts his hands on my back. I feel waves going through me longitudinally, as if my physical body itself is rippling – from the right side to the left. Then I feel my neck, head, spine straighten, re-aligned. I feel almost transparent too – like cloudy jelly. I can see the gateway ahead – I am so keen to go through it – Merlin has to call me back for my drink – we both laugh about that. The golden tankard is balanced on a mossy rock on the opposite side of the path to the great flower. The liquid is like water with fruit juice – but no fruit juice I have ever actually tasted before, delicious, cleansing.

At some point in these movements, I see the back of Merlin's cloak – and notice that it is different from what I saw before – in a much earlier meeting. This time there is no upside-down child me clinging there – but there are two women entwined, back view only, no faces, and right way up. They are obviously moving forwards together to some new place … the same place I am going, I guess, my higher-self blended with me like a dear sister, free!

Yes – I want to go though that gateway – "I am willing", I tell Merlin, "to do all that it requires of me, to be what is necessary, to commit myself to this new path. - I am willing to grow through love instead of struggle, to continue to grow, but to not forget my feminine side, to trust in the magic, and to honour my visions and be myself. I want to live this new way of being – be in touch with the present moment – and move forward."

I step through the gateway…. And beyond, there is a new land, a new page / place, to map out. "I can make this place anything I want!" I exclaim to myself, "I will write my own reality – I already am….."

I slowly wake up and stretch in my newly aligned body and my newly affirmed belief. I sit up and gaze around me with new shining eyes, and I know that things will be good.

Note – although Merlin is a fictional rather than a historical figure, the idea of him is deeply ingrained into our subconscious, and the archetype really works well.

Keywords – *Sister / Cool Wet Forest Trees – Leaves / Laughter / Freedom / New Fruit / Flowers /Water / Bird Sounds / Magic / Tranquil Pool / New Land – New Roots – New Growth / Grace / Pink Flower of Love squashes out any disease from within / Cleansing.*

Be patient and be humble
Close down very gently after meditation, too tightly will block energy. Trust & learn / Do not give away your power / Listen to your whispers from within.

Refresh yourself / **Take time to rest and play** / Use cycles / Be natural. Be playful too.

Fear is the lack of spiritual awareness / **Love is the greatest healing force of all.** Love can dissolve all fear.

Meditation increases the light, love, and level of spiritual energy for yourself, and for the whole planet.

Through the Mud

A line of robots,
we approach a wall of mud,
some of us
carrying flowers –
the others laugh
but when we enter that wall
it is the flowers
that will make us an ark
to carry us on through the darkness,
sailing through,
with our symbols the only light
until we fly
out over the fields
on the other side of midnight
and all our wires
and bits of metal fall off
and dive deep
beneath the deepest ocean –
and our souls are bright again,
so new and light
they shoot up –
up to plant our brilliant flowers
like stars
in the face of heaven.

From my book "BLUE BRIDGE"

Positive and Purposeful Living

There is much on my website to help – tools, inspiration, articles, guides, etc. The Stress Busting and Confirming Joy Guides should be particularly useful. Also the Meditation Guide and related Articles – Meditation is a most wonderful tool for almost anything. And there is a Mastery guide now too. All the tools can be used yourself and shared with friends.

Instead of letting our emotions run amok with our minds, we can use our minds as tools that allow us to build realities that serve us better, and we attract what we are meant to attract because we are so aware and self-empowered that we can choose most of the time.

You can literally direct your personal reality by adjusting your personal experience of the matrix to a level that suits you at that time, so that you can learn from that – and then move further – a bit like a climber bivouacking part way up a cliff face for a rest! Always remember that the climber does not see only the cliff, but also the sky above, and the view below.

Thinking positively begins really with rediscovering a sense of being grateful for what you do have – it could be good health, good husband, kids, friends, family, sense of identity, financial security, home, country, interesting job or studies, pets, hobbies, etc. Remember to use the affirmations in here too.

Once you show appreciation for something or someone, it or they tend to flourish more. If you are thinking about the good things, then your focus is on those. You tend to just get on then with enjoying the good things – it is that simple.

"The greatest discovery of my generation is that a human being can alter his life by altering his attitudes." – William James

"In the century now dawning, spirituality, visionary consciousness, and the ability to build and mend human relationships will be more important for the fate and safety of this nation than our capacity to forcefully subdue an enemy. **Creating the world we want is a much more subtle but more powerful mode of operation than destroying the one we don't want.**" – Marianne Williamson

"All speech, action, and behaviour are fluctuations of consciousness. All life emerges from, and is sustained in, consciousness. The whole universe is the expression of consciousness. The reality of the universe is one unbounded ocean of consciousness in motion." – Maharishi Mahesh Yogi

"Everything you see has its roots in the unseen world. The forms may change, yet the essence remains the same. Every wonderful sight will vanish; every sweet word will fade, but do not be disheartened, the source they come from is eternal, growing, branching out, giving new life and new joy. Why do you weep? The source is within you and this whole world is springing up from it." – Jelaluddin Rumi

"The process of Mastery is one of acceptance. It is a quiet embracing of what is. It is a non-resistance. It is a gentle walking into the moment, knowing that it holds for us, always, what is best for us all ways. Do you believe this? Then it is true." – Neale Donald Walsch

Enjoy it now, but do not fear endings, for there are always new beginnings, and when they come you can enjoy them all the more. Use whatever tools work for you. **Live your life on purpose – be who you mean to be.**

There is ecstasy in laughter, movement, stillness, gratefulness. There is a huge steadiness in balance. There is love and beauty all around us if we take the time to notice and celebrate the little details, to feel the grace and light, breathe, touch, play, and drink it in.

Life BY DESIGN – Walk through the gateway to a new and empowered you!

Decide what matters to you most, and choose to do it, then plan out how, but ask the universe to help with the general flow.

You can also use a life coach to help you plan out how to achieve things once you know what you want to achieve. Some life coaches can also help you find out what it might be that you want to achieve if you are not sure.

In any case, it is good if you can use the above phrases to jog your memory – to remind yourself that you certainly CAN decide to Live on Purpose and Design your own Life. Don't forget that you are the one in control. Sometimes there might be very difficult choices to make, but it is still in your power to make them. Even if some circumstances are beyond your control, it is how you respond to these that makes a huge difference.

Remind yourself that you can always learn something whatever the circumstances, and move on all the wiser. Because of the natural web of existence, there have to be shake-ups and balances along the way for life (at least in the physical sense) to be possible, and it is part of our empowerment to increase our understanding of that, and love life anyway, along with all its diverse ingredients.

tenderness

The Blue Bridge (title of one of my poetry collections)
could represent Communication by the way,
a skill we really need to develop better in all private & public situations,
as problems with this can cause so many bigger issues.
However, so long as you are at least prepared to listen,
to sit patiently with others and communicate
instead of reacting or running away,
then you are on a good path.

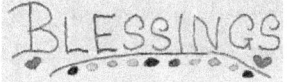

That takes us nicely into the next section:

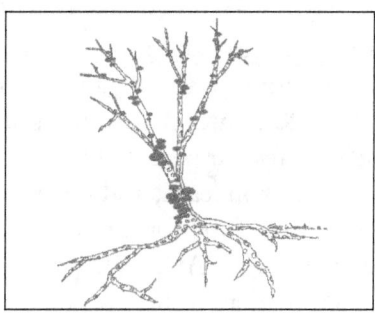

Trying to be TWO – (in Relationships)

We should be whole in ourselves before we can expect a balanced relationship.
     Ideally we need to learn to be who we really are first and then find a right relationship instead of expecting a relationship to fill gaps in our selves. If we approach relationship with a sense of need, then we are likely to fail because nobody else can be responsible for fulfilling some need for you. Neediness tends to be destructive in any relationship. People should trust each other and allow each other to be who they are, instead of trying to control them and make them into some idea of who they think they should be, or need them to be.
     Communication is vital. We can resolve all sorts of issues by being totally honest and keeping calm. We can ask the other to give us the chance to speak and give us a fair hearing, or we can write things down. We need to clearly focus on what matters most and seek honest resolutions without any attempt to emotionally manipulate, or throw in all sorts of extra agitations.
     We need not polarize towards one side or the other of ideas, such as if it is sexually wise to be liberal or conservative, for example – my folks taught me that sex is an important part of a relationship so you should know what it will be like before you marry someone. But, if you try out everyone you like you will get confused and not be ready when the right person does come along, so friendships are better until you are more sure. If you are going from one relationship to the next then how can you be free to meet the special one? Also, I notice that even people who think they are totally fine with very liberal ways of life, show physical symptoms of stress due to their bodies not entirely agreeing with their minds. And of course there is the threat of possible STD's, which would rather damage a relationship if brought in from outside. So ideally we should learn to be who we really are first and then find a right relationship, instead of expecting a relationship to fill gaps in our selves.
     Life is not black & white, it is many shades in-between, so you decide for yourself what your personal rules should be – and be prepared to change them as you learn, and never blame yourself for what you thought was right before, for that is what you thought then in the light of what you knew then. Also, remember to allow others the grace of this insight. Allow them to be who they choose to be at any moment on their own journey.

Many of us grew up not having been taught how to respect our own bodies. I knew how to respect my intelligence and was encouraged to be a free thinker, but I was not shown how important my body is. I used to give it away too easily to try to find love. But love does not come to one who does not know how to respect one's self, only people who use you, mistreat you, discard you, or those who try to subdue or control you. Once you wake up to the knowledge of your own beauty and the right to be treated like a jewel, then you find love. In the smile of the confident the eyes shine like diamonds because they know that truth. No man has a right to mistreat me, I choose only those who show the deepest respect, and that wisdom is reflected in his touch.

This is your mind and your body! Ask only for what you want. Do not throw caution to the wind and accept just any old thing. Have some respect for your self, and your right to be whole, and to be treated like a whole human with a heart full of wisdom. Fly like a bird on the wings of that wisdom from anyone who wants to harm you or cage you or pluck a single one of your beautiful feathers out.

Once you are in a fully balanced relationship you can certainly often feel as if you are one being, blended at many levels, but ultimately you are still physically separate and have to take responsibility for maintaining your own balances rather than depending on the other, and both parties share responsibility for nurturing the relationship and helping it to fulfil its potential. Both need to feel cherished.

I have **meditations for couples** in one of my guides, and use them in workshops. These can be extremely healing if you both intend to embark on a journey of discovery together, or a journey to renew your relationship, even in the face of great hurt. We can also always improve our communication skills.

We can of course use counsellors or other uninvolved specialists to help us resolve issues. This is not about the actual resolutions, it is more about getting help to allow you to communicate fully, to mediate if need be, and ultimately you are the ones who come up with any solutions.

Barbara Wren says "Every time we go outside ourselves to seek our wisdom, it immediately becomes someone else's wisdom and not our own. We are not able to contribute our own uniqueness, our own wisdom, to the universal picture, the greater whole. We need to live our uniqueness because this is what creates the order of the greater whole. As soon as we cease to look inside and instead look outside, there is mediocrity, standardization and control across the globe. The answer to any question you might ask is within you."

So, a good counsellor will not try to tell you what to do, but simply help you to discover how to best help yourself. A good healer too, will help you use your own connections with your own body, your higher self, and the wider universe, to find your own unique balance. Both will ultimately empower you to live a more fulfilled life where you are also better able to interact with others and cope with things out in the world around you. They will help you overcome any block to proceeding with your personal life's journey.

Be aware of / open to possibilities – don't limit yourself with either/or thinking.

We should not wish to gravitate towards one pole or another as those are the extremities. We should ideally be somewhere in-between and make allowances for everyone else to be somewhere in-between as well – anywhere they wish to be – that is appropriate for them at the current point on their journeys. If we are thinking that things have to be either/or, then we are shutting out the magic of life's natural evolution, and trapping ourselves in separateness and limitation. Thinking in black and white or in boxes always excludes us from the amazing possibilities (or colours) outside the boxes. Life definitely overflows any attempt to put things in boxes.

There isn't a good side and a bad side of you or of anybody, so there's no need to be at war with anyone or anything at all. All we are is a bunch of dozy people in the process of waking up. All we really need to do is try gently to be open to continuing that process. It's no good getting worked up about stuff – it's better to relax and laugh at our mistakes, then figure out how to move on.

Practicing tenderness and massage

Showing tenderness in a relationship keeps reminding us of the positive love in the world as a whole and in our hearts.

There are exercises in my guide to help bring couples very close so that they can share an absolutely pure relationship. They are based on open communication, which can only be done with truly opened hearts.

Massage is a wonderful tool for two people who wish to learn to trust each other at a very deep level, and to deepen each other's faith in their partner's love for them. Partners need to respect each other's feelings and boundaries or limits, as well as their bodies, so you also need to talk openly and listen fully. Massage also enables you to process the toxins of trapped emotions, and start afresh.

Light up your Life

TENDERNESS *(from my book "SPIRIT SONGS")*

```
          D            G
Hold me, stroke me, / touch me tender
          D      G lo         A
Like no other / sun gave me its / light

          D      G hi         A
Like no other / stars have kissed my / eyes
          D      G lo         D       A lo
Like no other / planets ever / spun inside my / head

          D      G lo         A
Like no other / wind blew its own / breath
          D      G hi         D       A
Like no other / water sang its / song to me / before

          D      G lo         D       A
Like no other / earth - cradled / me - in its / arms
          D      G lo         hi    A hi
Like no other / tree - held me to its / heart

   hi  D     G hi           D       A
Like no other / bird - gave to / me its wings / before
          D      G lo         A
Like no other / kitten shared its / licks
          D      G lo         A
Like no other / cloud gave me its / lips
          D      G hi         D          A
Like no other / moon laid its ca / ress upon my / skin
          D      G lo         A
Like no other / grass has shared its / dreams
```

```
     D      G lo        A lo
Like no other / leaves have ever / li-ist-ened

  hi  D     G hi           D        A
Like no other / flo-ow-ers showed / me-ee their / co-o-lours
        D      G lo            A
Like no other / God showed me his / love
         D      G lo          A   D
Like no other / God showed me his / lo-o- / ove
```

FLY *(from my book "SPAN")*

Delicate, butterfly winged, we vainly push against the sky, each trying to find our place. Yes, we are going to die, let's not beat about the bush. Maybe today, maybe tomorrow. Maybe many years from now. Meanwhile, we have someone who loves us, someone to love. Surely there is no need to hesitate.

OBSERVATION *(from my book "SPAN")*

So, we may not be able to explain the world. Not exactly. But we CAN accept it, and love it. We CAN turn our faces to the light and examine the minutest details simply for the sake of it. We CAN live lives of joy and purpose. We are all part of one whole. Take comfort in this: Almost every one of us is capable of holding a cup to another's lips without our hands shaking.

Laughter, and Acting as if ……

In her book *Embracing Uncertainty*, Susan Jeffers says – "I believe the Laughing Buddha represents the inner intelligence that lives within us all. He represents the part of us that is in tune with the Grand Design. He doesn't try to control the chaos. Instead, he listens and moves comfortably within the chaos as the world unfolds around him. He stays open to a constant flow of 'joyous survival' versus 'turbulent survival'. He makes us realise that we can't get rid of the chaos but we can get very creative with the turmoil. We are all the creators of how we want to see this world."

She also suggests that when we are troubled by something, we ask ourselves what the Laughing Buddha would tell us, or even pretend we are a Laughing Buddha!

As a life coach I sometimes tell people they can enhance their ability to achieve a desired state if they actually act as if they are already there. Sometimes just doing it brings surprising results. Even if you pretend you are sleeping, you might actually drift off.

Your mind is not in control of you, it is a tool for you to use for your benefit.

Remember to think positively as much as you can, even if you just start with a few moments each morning, and focus on being grateful for what you do have.

Please also see the section of our Confirming Your Joy Guide called "Choice and Positive Thinking". Various other sections in the same guide are also very useful here – "Living in the Now & the Flow", "No Fear", and "Freedom."

Care for Yourself :

Eat well, drink lots of water, exercise appropriately, stand tall, sleep well, dream! Get to really understand you body and what is good for it. You can do the same with your mind and emotions, observe how you think and react to things and figure out why, then you can learn to make any adjustments you may wish to.

Act As if :

Fake it! You are beautiful all over – dress as if you are brilliant, fabulous – walk as if you are – smile as if you know you are – love as if you are – sing as if you are – dance as if you are – and you soon will be! You are already, it's just that you have to act it until you believe it. We all are – why should we not be? It is a denigration of your inner self to not accept this – every single one of us is beautiful in our own unique way.

Use Visualisations, such as – "I radiate vitality & grace".

Be Inspired, Mature, & Shine :

When you shine, you give others permission to do so. They love being around you, you are an example to them. Your love and light dissolves their fears. If they were worried about what others might think, or afraid of taking chances, or of being themselves, then you will be an inspiration to them.

Enjoy your Relationships!

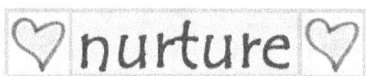

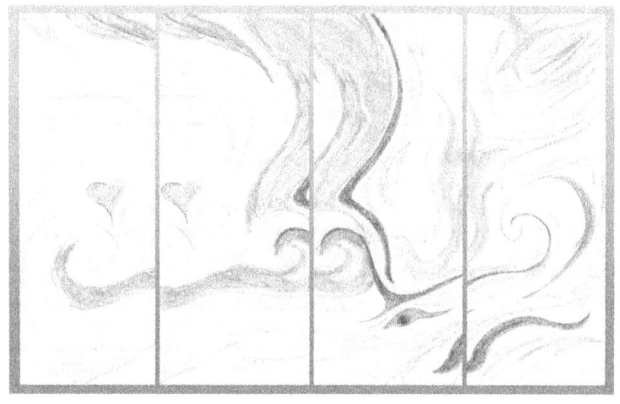

MANY – BUT STILL ONE -
(A place in Local & Global Communities.)

Polarities are inherently paradoxical. These opposites cannot exist without each other, therefore they form a unity.

As a person, you exist within the life stream (of pure consciousness). As awareness, the life stream/dream arises within you (forming your reality). As a consciously evolving Being you direct your life/dream (and continually review it).

You can switch your focus between the first two, yet still retain a peripheral awareness of the other. You dance between them, you weave your path of life between them.

So, while living in the matrix that supports separateness, you remain aware of oneness – the ultimate unity and balance of the polarities.

Our goal is not a fixed state of consciousness, but a fluid state – so we can be in whatever state best suits us as needed.

We are firmly engaged in being here and experiencing this life (being in the dream), but at the same time we are aware of the process of the life dream arising within us (making the dream). We are also consciously watching, analysing, learning, changing our responses or intentions wherever we choose to – unfolding our being-ness as we best see fit from moment to moment, and thus fine-tuning the dream.

So, what we are being is a separate entity, as we need to in our day-to-day lives, yet we are simultaneously tuned into a sense of unity, and trying to live in harmony with that. We call it into our focus when it can help us move forward better (in its flow), and we answer to it when we need to respond appropriately.

Often even in our day-to-day lives, we are part of a couple, family, team, or even country, so we need to be aware of the wider needs of the couple or group and keep a good balance on behalf of all members. It can be very helpful to deliberately call in a sense of unity prior to a planning meeting or discussion, asking for harmony, lightness and grace to guide and aid you for the optimum good of all.

There have been sections on communication with colleagues, friends, family, partners, etc in this book and there is more in my other materials, which will all hopefully be of use too. I think that if we could all manage to communicate well, we could overcome most of humanity's problems. This of course includes our leaders, but it needs to come from the grassroots up because we need our leaders to listen to us and properly represent us.

Currently they cannot do this because the increase in legally enshrined privileges that protect the interests of corporations, allows the powerful few to have undue control over our political representatives, and our media. (They also control our financial systems and most of our supplies, and can therefore manipulate our economic and social situations to suit their own ends.) [Individuals may think they are responsibly working towards the best interests of their businesses and their clients as a whole - until one day they realise that there is some whole other agenda being perpetrated in the top echelons – usually primarily with the aim of making the top people richer at the expense of everyone else, and the environment.]

We should not be afraid to speak out, but to communicate effectively we need to speak clearly about what is most important, not just babble incessantly about anything and everything. To call for big change we need to communicate with others and work together in an organised fashion to achieve it. If we can be mature, and insistent (firm), in our communication then perhaps our nations can grow up to become nations working for the good of humanity both in their own locality and as a whole.

A word of warning though: please do be sure not to sign up to any false call to unity, led by those wanting control, probably tricking you though fear to sacrifice personal freedoms for example, in exchange for things like protection & supplies. If we lose freedoms it also means losing so much more - choices, individuality, along with our diverse emotional, spiritual and philosophical natures - and this would completely alter the definition of conscious humanity. There isn't much consciousness in slave / master situations. Please, only respond to what feels right, sings in your conscious heart. Trust your instincts. Whether we like it or not, there is big change afoot.

Try to find out about things instead of just accepting what is happening around you. Try to act responsibly for the optimum good of all. **Keep your awareness and your intentions fine-tuned and you should do yourself and all of us proud.**

Do come and network with us in our facebook open group "Back to The Garden" - help play a part in everything going on! We also have a website called backtothegarden.org.uk

Live lightly now and remember, we are all interconnected in this web of life.

The universe feeds us freedom food in a continual flow of discovery, which is the essence of life, or the life force itself.

We accept it gratefully, trying to be aware enough to become our true deep selves in every way we can.

We are responsible for our own personal journey, which is always again part of the journey of the whole, creating and evolving eternally

If you align your physical & mental (logical/emotional) self with your core self (or soul being), then you will know your personal path, and find ways to follow it to fulfillment.

You can learn how to best nurture your body, plus train your mind as an empowering tool to enhance your overall balance, strength, and unique skills, so that you achieve your goals, as well as optimise your well-being.

"What if everything were information –
physical codes of DNA
and spiritual codes of soul –
a blueprint for your creation?

It allows you to become
an infant human . . . .
We then receive added information
from our parents and others
to help us develop –
until we begin to add
information from our own experience,
and build ego and identity.

We continue to learn from others,
but we can believe or not believe
things we are told;
and we can seek out other information
as we mature.
It is up to us to choose
who we are being
in relation to the information
swarming round us.

We can align ourselves
with whatever works best for us;
but we should never give up seeking,
growing, adjusting.
We are not helpless.
Our reality is the result
of our total resourced information,
which is the basis of what we become.

Be aware that this is always changeable.
Anytime you choose
to create a different picture
you can find tools and resources
to help you sketch it out –
then paint in the details.
You can map and build
to your hearts content –
be the architect of your own being.

It is your consciousness
to do with what you will."

"Breathe in deeply –
Breathe out completely.
Continue to do this
as you connect with
the Universal Breath,
the Divine Flow
that sustains us.
Know that you are loved –
Breathe in that love,
and breathe out your own love
to share with the world.
Continue to breathe
love in and out
to sustain your wellness.
Take your consciousness
through your body
and direct your breath
to remove any stress
and boost your energy.
Remain in balance
so that you can give
your unique gifts to the world.
Breathe the love in and out
whenever you need to
find calm and sustenance.
Choose health, peace,
whatever else it is you want,
and breathe it into your being."

This poem - NAMING THE EARTH – *was published on Surrey Libraries website for National Poetry Day 2015 with it's theme of LIGHT. It was also published prior to that in the Paddington International Festival 2001 Anthology.*

And the world will be born again
in circles of steaming breath
and beams of light
as each one of us directs
our inner eye
upon its name.

Hear the cry of wings,
the sigh of leaves and grass,
smell the new sweet mist rising
as the pathway is cleared at last.

Stones stand ready -
they have known
since ages and ages ago
that they were not alone.
Water carries the planet's energy
into skies and down
to earth and bones.

The cold parts steadily
as we come together,
bodies and hearts warm,
hands tingling.
We are silent
but our eyes are singing.

We look, we feel, we know,
we trust each other's souls,
we have no need to speak.
Not now, but later,
when the time is right,
the name will ring

within the iron core
of each other's listening -
and the very earth's being.

Every creature, every plant,
will hear it calling,
tolling like a bell -
a sound we've always felt
but never dared to hope
to hear reverberating -
true at last, at every level
of existence.

The poets come together
to open the intimate centre.
Believe - in life and air -
breathe the light itself,
for these are the energies
and rhythms that we need
to see, to touch, to reach,
to identify, to say, the NAME.

Colours on your skin
fuse and dissolve -
leave the river clean
for pure space and time
to enter and flow in.

We all become one fluid stream
of stillness and motion,
of flaring thought
pulses discovering
weird pools and twists within

where darkness hides
from the flames in our eyes
but will not snare us.

We probe deeper still,
journeying towards a unity
which will be more raw
and yet also more formed
than anything written
or spoken before.

Our fragile bodies
fall away -
and the trees,
and the roots of trees,
guide us -
lead us away
from the faces we remember
seeing in the mirror each day -

into an ocean
of dreams
seething with warmth,
love,
where the beginning
is real,

ripe, evolving

*And the world is born again
in circles of steaming breath
and beams of light.*

An ache -
a signal -

a trembling moment -
and the time is right
to say the name.

We sing as one whole
voice of the universal -
all the words, the names
of every tiny thirsting thing,
and they ring out together
as one sound,
one energy, one sense,
one vibration, one breath.

And the world listens,
beats, shines, glows -
IS -
Exists!

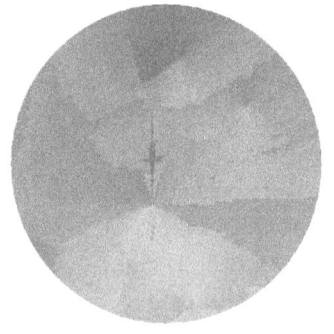

END NOTES - **ESCAPING THE "MATRIX"**

This book shows how we can evolve through our understanding and **awareness**.

Once we can see how the system of paradoxes works, to enable us to experience existence in this physical world, we can accept this "matrix" for what it is - using it, but at the same time moving outside its limits as well.

At a certain level of existence this "matrix" is absolutely essential to our survival, but our spirits and our higher minds do not need to be trapped in the mesh, they can flutter free - perhaps just for short moments to start with, but more and more, as we are able to hold ourselves steady, and stop allowing other people and events to pull our strings as if we were puppets.

Not that the everyday does not matter, of course it does - just that if you can grasp this idea, then you can live on a LIGHTER level, where you use techniques and awareness to remind yourself that there *are* different levels of existence, some more evolved than others. We are each at the level appropriate to our learning at any given time (so there should be no judgement of yourself or of others).

Being aware enough, enables us to heighten our level of consciousness more easily. Using our minds as **tools** helps raise awareness. We can see the world in a more detached way, be **objective** about things, instead of reacting emotionally. So we avoid getting caught up in the mess of greed, fear, anger, manipulation, deceit, and war.

You can still experience life fully, in fact more fully, because you choose what is important for you to focus on, and stop wasting energy in pointless arguments, worry, or distress. Instead you can focus with peace, grace, and joy, on bringing more positive things into your life, and on **exploring** the amazing delights and possibilities on offer.

You can make *your* choices of how to live in a much more conscious way. **What you make of your life is your personal evolution, and you can guide yourself in a very aware way.**

If you are clear about what you **intend** to achieve, and focus on that, then that result is what is naturally attracted to you, whereas if you focus on the negative then that is what is attracted to you. Whatever thoughts, feelings, and actions you project are reflected back to you.

The beliefs you express define your reality, so don't let the limitations of what you are taught, or the confines of other people's constructs, restrict your personal world! Chris said *"Remember when you were a child and you felt sure you could fly – that is a good feeling to have."* You actually have access to unlimited information & knowledge to empower you. **The process of discovery keeps adding to your energy, and everything expands exponentially.**

All the information in the collective unconscious (and the matrix) stems from past experiences only; so if we step beyond that, into higher consciousness, we can then accept the power of extra-sensory abilities, the concept of inner worlds and undiscovered dimensions, etc, and the idea of huge positive change.

So why not make your life more newly conscious? Why not make miracles a part of your reality? Open to the flow of universal energy that you are already connected to, and enjoy the journey! Anything you can conceive of is already part of you, so it's up to you what you manifest, and what you become. **Conscious Evolution is a process of continually becoming, through informed and self-managed choices.** In each moment we become continually new because we re-define ourselves with each new piece of information, each experience, and each thought. If all our thoughts and responses are as conscious as we can make them, then we are being our highest possible self in each moment.

I hope this book has given you a lot of useful ideas, information, and tools to empower and inspire you to do that **lovingly, yet firmly,** on the personal, and also on the community and global levels.

It is not selfish to spend time on your own development, because the more you become your highest possible self, the more you can help others, and the planet. However, **humility is part of the process.** Your detachment from the matrix is also a detachment from ego. Okay, so you can't *entirely* escape the matrix, or the ego, but you use them just for the basic, necessary, purposes of physical survival here. All other levels of yourself can break free, and sometimes you will need to stand up for your right to truly do this, although you can always choose to do so from the warmest, gentlest depths of your heart. (Assertion is not meant to be aggressive.)

The way you conduct yourself gives a message to others about who you choose to be. The state of your personal consciousness always affects those around you, as well as the collective state everywhere, so what better way to bring more good stuff into the world? You can focus it wherever you wish.

As John Lennon said, "Evolution and all hopes for a better world rest in the fearlessness and open-hearted vision of people who embrace life". Well, it is your life to embrace, and I trust you will define how you want it to be, for each one of you, and for all of us.

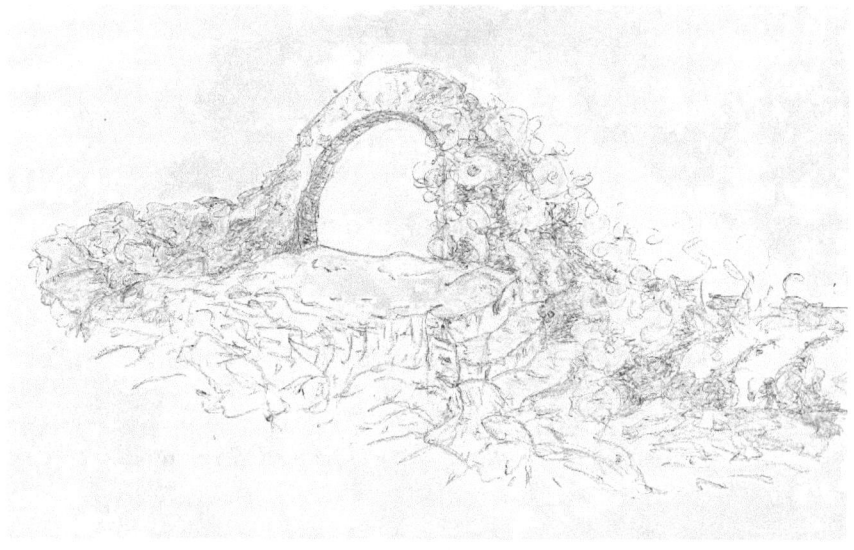

Enter unto your deeper self, then arise
and step out into the clear clean light
of new becomings.

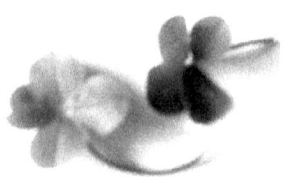

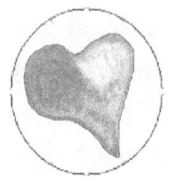

Information about Julia Woodman's other books is on her website, plus on Amazon.

There are several other books of this nature, plus quite a bit of poetry (as Jay Woodman).

Julia is also writing a novel, which will probably be the first of several.

www.ingramcontent.com/pod-product-compliance
Lightning Source LLC
LaVergne TN
LVHW051555070426
835507LV00021B/2597